A Better Work

Books by Michael Jenet

FICTION
(THE DI SCOTTE MYSTERIES)
Trouble Comes In Threes
A Trio of Trouble

SELF IMPROVEMENT/BUSINESS
MOTIVESTIONS - The Missing Key to Living Your Best Life
(*O*riginally published as: *ASK: The Questions to Empower Your Life*)

(THE BETTER SERIES)
A Better Life
A Better Work

CONTRIBUTING AUTHOR
Peanut's Legacy
Imagine: 29 Days To A Better You

A Better Work

MICHAEL JENET

Guide Point North Publishing
Colorado, U.S.A.

Guide Point North Publishing
An imprint of Journey Institute Press,
a division of 50 in 52 Journey, Inc.
journeyinstitutepress.org

Library of Congress Control Number: Available Upon Request
Names: Jenet, Michael
Title: A Better Work
Description: Colorado: Guide Poiont North Publishing, 2025

Identifiers: ISBN 978-1-964754-49-9 (hardcover)
ISBN 978-1-964754-50-5 (paperback)
ISBN 978-1-964754-51-2 (ebook/kindle)

Subjects: BISAC:
BUSINESS & ECONOMICS / Leadership |
BUSINESS & ECONOMICS / Management |
BUSINESS & ECONOMICS / Workplace Culture

First Edition
Printed in the United States of America

1 3 7 14 21 39 48 58 61 88

This book was typeset in EB Garamond / Dancing Script
Editing by Jessica Medberry, InkWhale Editorial LLC.
Cover design by WiggleB Studios

For Dafna, who spoke this book into existense.
Work and play would never be the
same without you.
AOTAOT.

Chapter 1
The Bridge

Tonight is the night I'm going to die.

Don't feel sorry for me; I deserve it. In fact, I should have been dead long before now.

What I have done—or better yet, what I have not done—has caused great harm to many people. I cannot change the past, but perhaps tonight, with my death, I can help create a better future. For them at least.

It's a pity, really, I think. *This used to be one of my favorite cities.*

I'm standing on London Bridge, which most people confuse with Tower Bridge, though the two look nothing alike. London Bridge is one bridge over. You can see Tower Bridge lit up in all its glory from the side opposite where I'm standing, the side where tourists take photos from. Not this late, of course—or early, depending on your point of view. Especially as it's currently drizzling rain. I'm staring into the rushing water of the River Thames below. Ink-black pools of water swirl by in the clouded moonlight.

I'm leaning against the concrete sections that make up the parapet on the side of the bridge. There's a metal railing at the top. The parapet is in sections, little concrete stations where you can see through the gaps that there's a large body of water on the other side, as though being on a bridge wasn't enough of a clue. The concrete is covered with polished granite panels. The parapet's noncontinuous nature seems appropriate, given that London Bridge is the only hollow bridge crossing the Thames. I'm not sure why it pops into my head, but I suddenly remember that the bridge also has heated pavement, which is handy should the weather turn icy.

"Tonight's the night!" I yell into the night. My voice quickly lost in the brisk February air. It's Wednesday. Quite late, I think, though I've lost track of time.

I hear voices behind me. "Shhh, he's drunk," a man's voice says.

I turn around, and the motion makes my head ache. A man and a woman move quickly past. She is looking over her shoulder at me. He puts his arm protectively around her and hastily urges her to move on.

I dare say they're right, though I moved well beyond drunk some hours ago. I am now well and truly plastered. I'm feeling quite sorry for myself, but it's more than that.

I am miserable. I am hopeless. I am despondent. What's that French saying? *Je suis désolé?* I am desolate! Then again, I'm not sure that's right; it's been a long time since I learned the phrase in high school French class.

I thought I had a chance to make things right with this trip to London, but even that has been a failure. I climb over the railing awkwardly, almost falling off without even trying. I'm not that fond of heights, and my heart races as I grip the cold railing behind me.

I cling to the railing, and the irony isn't completely lost on me, despite my alcohol-muddled brain, that I'm attempting to commit suicide. I don't much like the idea of drowning, but the fact is I can't think of another way to do it. I'm certainly not going to slit my wrists and watch as my heart pumps blood out before my eyes. Shooting myself isn't realistic either, as guns are difficult to come by in England. Poison also doesn't seem like a possibility. I wouldn't know what poison to get, even if I knew where to get it.

I hadn't planned on killing myself until I started crossing the bridge on my way back to the hotel. It suddenly seemed like the perfect answer to my troubles and those of the many people whose lives I've ruined.

The man doesn't make a sound. I'm not even aware of his presence beside me until he speaks. His voice startles me so badly I nearly jump from fright.

"It won't kill you, you know," he says. "The fall, I mean."

I momentarily let go with my right arm as my head jerks in the direction of his voice, but then quickly reach back and re-establish my grip on the railing. The swift turn of my head sends fireworks off inside my mind, and I nearly let go right then and there. "What?" I ask, grimacing.

He is only a few feet away from me, not really close enough to touch. A man in his mid-thirties. I squint in the dim light. I think slightly older than me and dressed oddly. Through my bloodshot eyes, I see he is wearing some sort of billowing white shirt with a black vest over it. *Isn't he cold?* He has long, light-blond hair and piercing blue eyes. His expression seems more curious than alarmed, as if standing on a bridge in the middle of the night talking to someone who is about to jump off was an everyday occurrence.

He looks down into the water and then over at me. "The fall," he repeats matter-of-factly. "It's not far enough to kill you." He continues speaking before I can form words in my sluggish mouth. "I mean, you might sprain something or, I daresay, maybe even break your foot on the impact, but it's not nearly far enough to kill you. Most people think hitting the water at this height is like jumping off a diving board, but this is quite a bit higher. It will hurt, don't get me wrong, but as I say, it won't kill you."

I'm sure I'm giving him an incredulous look, as if to say, "What are you prattling on about, and why don't you just go away?"

If he notices, he doesn't show it. Instead, he looks down into the water and says, "It's also much too deep for you to hit bottom, so that won't do it either."

I formulate enough thought in my molasses-laden synapses to put together a reply. "Look, I don't mean to be rude, but can you please just leave me alone?"

At least, that's what I want to say. I have no idea what comes out of my mouth instead, and it probably just sounds like gibberish from a defeated drunk clinging haphazardly to the side of a bridge.

My new companion ignores it. "Don't you worry though," he says, looking straight at me and smiling. "You'll die all right." Then he adds, "The water will do it."

Again, I command the muscles in my mouth to obey the mashed-together thoughts in my brain. "What do you mean?" I ask, though what I hear come out sounds more like, "Waadaayaa meeeeeaaannnn?" and is much louder than I intended.

"First," he begins, "that water's practically freezing, so when you hit, it will feel as though you're hitting cement." He pauses, looking to see if the words are getting through the alcohol and into my brain. "That's when you'll likely sprain or break something. Next will come the cold. A cold that is nothing like anything else you've ever felt. It will instantly penetrate your clothes, and the shock will expel all the air from your lungs. It will paralyze your muscles instantly, and you won't be able to move your arms or legs."

Again, he pauses, this time leaning forward slightly to look at me as my head sways in front of him. I want to tell him I can understand him, but I am too busy focusing on his words. It takes all the energy I have to make out what he is saying, and I am rapt with attention.

Satisfied that I seemed to process his tale, he continues, "At first your buoyancy will want to bring you back up to the surface, and your fight-or-flight systems will take over, such that you will probably be able to get a fresh lungful of air when your head breaks the surface." He indicated a swooping motion with his hand, first down and then arcing until it pumped straight up, indicating my head breaking above the waves.

"That," he says solemnly, "will be the last breath of fresh air you will get."

I'm not sure I like the tone of his voice at this point, but I am processing too slowly to stop him from continuing. "Inevitably," he says, his eyebrows rising slightly, "your body weight and wet clothes, along with the current of the river, will bring you back down under the water."

He let the weight of his words sink in. "That's when the water will kill you."

I let go with my left hand and suddenly my body swings out over the abyss below. My right hand instinctively clutches the metal railing tightly, and my momentum swings me around until I can grab the railing with my left hand again. Now I am almost face-to-face with my oddly dressed storyteller, my back toward the expanse of the river.

He doesn't flinch. He doesn't move a muscle except to turn his head ever so slightly to look me right in the eye, now mere inches away. "Your body will try to breathe eventually," he says, his eyes dark in the dim light and yet still piercingly clear. His voice is crisp in the cool night air. "But there won't be any air to take in." Then he adds, "Only the cold, putrid water of the river."

I can feel my stomach beginning to lurch—whether from the effect of his words or the sloshing of alcohol in my gut, I couldn't tell you. Likely both.

He slaps the railing with his left hand. "Anyway, I just wanted you to know." Then half turning to go, he adds, "You know, the last thing that will go through your mind is that you're dying from a mouthful of some of the most soiled and rotten water, infested with rank sewage and rubbish, as it goes rushing into your lungs."

That does it. The bile in my stomach suddenly comes rushing up my esophagus, and I lean over the railing and am sick over the walkway.

I attempt to climb back over the railing as my stomach lurches and much of what I've been pouring down my throat over the past several hours comes back up. All while I cling to the side of one of the most famously named bridges in the world.

***

I don't remember how I got back to my hotel or, for that matter, how I ended up in bed with no shirt but still wearing my pants and socks. When I opened my eyes to the blinding light that was streaming through the window, my first thought was that I must be dead and that this was what hell felt like.

My entire body ached, but the sensation in my head was beyond anything I'd ever felt before. Like being in a vise, the handle turning ever so slightly inch by inch, while loud music blared, complete with thumping bass and screeching guitar solos.

The pain was so bad I almost couldn't register the knife-like jabs that assaulted my optic nerves as my eyes shut themselves quickly to keep out the pain.

Too late. Much to the disbelief of the infinitesimally small part of my brain that could still process actual thought, the pain got worse. I felt more than consciously heard myself groan out loud, but that only made the cacophony inside my head worse.

I wanted to be sick again and tried to move, wanting to reach the bathroom. I made it as far as the edge of the bed before retching once more.

The next few hours were beyond miserable. The stench from the floor did nothing to help the nausea, but I was in too much pain to do anything about it. Every sound was amplified by a magnitude of ten, from the traffic on the street below to the footsteps of people in the hallway.

When someone from housekeeping knocked on the door, I thought the sound was moving across the room and banging into my head like a wave of electricity.

It was well into the late afternoon before I got to the bathroom and into a shower. I stayed under the running water long after the hot water became cold until I suddenly remembered the man on the bridge. I shuddered and turned off the water as his words about the icy-cold Thames reverberated in my still-aching head.

Was he responsible for getting me back to my hotel? How had he known which hotel to take me to and which room I was in, if I had passed out? I couldn't remember anything beyond being sick on the bridge. The memory caused my stomach to lurch so quickly that I had to take deep gulps of air to prevent a repeat performance.

I wrapped a towel around myself, then left the bathroom and walked into the adjoining anteroom of my suite, avoiding the mess I'd made next to the bed. I called the front desk and asked them to send someone up to clean my room. I felt guilty about the poor soul who would walk in and find the state of it, but as I threw on some jeans and a shirt to escape being there when they arrived, there was a knock on my door.

That was quick, I thought.

I plodded to the door and opened it, trying to formulate the story I could give to explain the disaster that had resulted from my last five days in the room.

The person standing on the other side of the threshold was the last person I expected to see.

Martin Wesland. Venture capitalist, entrepreneur, and the principal investor who had helped me launch my company. I hadn't spoken to him for over three years.

When I set out with two friends to build a company around an idea for a revolutionary mobile app, it was Martin Wesland who had seen the potential and agreed to take a risk on three college kids. His gamble had paid off, and we were able to pay his investment back in record time. In fact, our success was so rapid that my two friends broke off to form another venture.

We parted ways amicably, but I wanted to continue building the company and began hiring developers to work on more and more apps. Looking back, that's when things started to unravel.

"Hello, Ethan," Martin said.

"Martin," I said, surprised. "What . . . what are you doing here?"

"Aren't you going to invite me in?"

I really didn't have much of a choice. "Oh . . . sorry, sure," I said weakly, stepping back from the threshold.

He surveyed the anteroom full of old takeaway boxes and empty bottles strewn over the furniture and floor. When he looked at me, his expression was somewhere between concern and disapproval. I was too embarrassed to explain. Instead, I said, "Housekeeping is on its way up."

He nodded silently.

Martin and I had always had an understanding between us, as if somehow we could communicate even when no words were exchanged. When my friends and I had pitched him on the company, it wasn't so much what had come out of my mouth that had sealed the deal, but rather some moments when he and I had made eye contact in silence.

I cleared off a chair for Martin to sit in and sat on the edge of my bed. "How did you know I was here?"

"Sam called me."

Sam was my second-in-command at the office. I had no idea the two had kept in touch.

"Apparently, you've been MIA for the better part of a week," Martin said, and before I could answer he continued, "and from what I gather, even before that, you've been checked out for months."

My defenses wanted to stand up and protest. To refute, to deny, to explain, but when I opened my mouth, nothing came out.

"You don't deny it, then," he said matter-of-factly.

I simply shook my head slowly. There was no point in trying to deny the truth.

"The thing is, Ethan," he said suddenly, "I feel partly responsible."

I frowned and tilted my head slightly. He leaned forward with his forearms against his thighs and looked me straight in the eye. "That's why I'm here. To help you."

I couldn't believe what he was saying. Martin had been the first to invest in the company when we'd started, and when his belief had paid off, he had brought together a small group of investors who gave us a second infusion when we wanted to expand. Our small company grew to ten, then twenty, and flourished to the current count of sixty-three employees. We had even received offers from rival companies that wanted to merge or buy us outright. The operative word there being "had."

I'd steadfastly refused, wanting my company to stay independent and not sell out to some larger corporation. It was a decision I regretted as I watched our business and our products steadily decline in the increasingly competitive market of application development.

"When Sam called, I looked into what's been going on," Martin said, shaking me back to reality from my trip down memory lane. "When you came back to me after your second year and asked if I would be interested in helping you with the expansion, I jumped at the chance."

He was still leaning forward in his chair, his voice soft and almost wistful, but the look on his face was serious. "I knew you had a good thing going, and more of a good thing would only mean a good return on my investment." He paused before adding, "And it was."

"But," he continued, straightening in his chair and holding his palms face up in a gesture that what he was about to say was obvious, "too much of a good thing isn't always a good thing, is it?"

I got up and stood by the window. I looked out at the traffic moving in the early evening light as commuters and tourists in cars, double-decker buses, and black cabs made their way across London below me. I didn't know how to respond.

"You have a brilliant mind, Ethan," he said gently, "and I know that the work you do is great work." He waited until I turned to look at him before he continued. When he did, there was an almost apologetic note in his voice. "It just didn't occur to me you wouldn't know how to run a business."

This time, my defenses jumped in before I could stop them. "Look," I said, my tone much harsher than I expected, "this isn't all my fault."

Martin looked at me quizzically, one eyebrow rising slightly.

"We have some great products," I said quickly, sweeping my arms wide to the scene out the window, "and if these people would only open their stupid minds, they would see that what we have to offer is better than anything else out there."

I was gaining steam, and now that I had an audience, all the reasoning and excuses and self-pity I had kept inside of me for months came pouring out. I rambled for a long time. Martin sat patiently and waited for me to get it all out.

I knew long before I was finished that my barrage of inane reasoning was nothing more than a childish tirade, but I couldn't restrain myself. When I finally ran out of things to say, I simply stopped in the middle of a sentence and turned back to the window, unsure of what my last train of thought had been.

Minutes passed. Neither of us spoke a word.

Finally, Martin rose from his chair and walked over to stand beside me.

"Ethan," he said, his voice gravely low and serious. He didn't look at me; he simply stared out the window. "You have three choices." He held up one finger as he said, "You can continue to blame everyone else and wait for the company to implode." He held up a second finger. "You can wallow in self-pity and drink yourself into a stupor while the company dies around you." Then, as he held up the third finger, he said, "Or you can grab on to a life preserver and start swimming."

I found his statements ironic, given the number of water references that had been clanging around in my mind in the last twenty-four hours, but I didn't have the mental energy to mention it. I was emotionally, physically, mentally, and in all other ways exhausted. I stood and stared out across the urban landscape of London. Tears leaked from my eyes, burning as they slowly slid down my cheeks. My voice, when it finally came, was high-pitched and trembling. "I don't know what to do."

Again, there was silence as Martin stared steadily out the window beside me. Then he looked over at me, his eyes kind and caring. The same look he had given me the first time he had said he would take a chance on me. It wasn't just about his investment or his excitement about a business opportunity. He had told me that more than the numbers or business plans, he often relied on his gut to tell him what to do, and his gut told him I was a good guy worth taking a risk on.

I had been embarrassed then. Now, as I saw that same look of belief, all I felt was shame. Finally, he reached into his pocket and said simply, "I know you feel lost." He pulled out a card, laid it down on the windowsill between us, and added, "But she can help you."

Then, without another word, he patted me on the shoulder, turned, and walked out of the room, the harsh click of the door as it slammed shut echoing in the silence.

I looked down at the card. Below two lines of printed text, in what I recognized as Martin's script, he had written *Tomorrow, 9am* and the name of a café a few blocks from my hotel.

I looked at the first line of the printed text: Life Prism Institute.

The second line read simply: VIOLET.

Chapter 2
Violet

I spent a restless night, with odd dreams of jumping off bridges, cliffs, and even the top of the Eiffel Tower before waking up and taking a shower. I'd shaved half-heartedly and put on a clean, if not slightly wrinkled, shirt from my suitcase. I contemplated putting on a suit but couldn't muster up the energy. I settled on a pair of mostly clean black slacks and a button-down shirt, then grabbed my coat and trudged down the four blocks from my hotel to the café.

I sat at a table just inside the door with my iced mocha and surveyed the room to see if there was a woman by herself that I had missed when I first walked in. I saw only a schoolgirl of maybe fifteen or sixteen who was texting on her phone with earbuds in her ears.

Several people were in line or had come and gone in the few minutes I had been there, but no one paid the slightest attention to me.

I had arrived ten minutes early, and each time a woman approached the door, I wondered if it would be her. At one minute to nine, a group of three entered. Two women and a man. The first woman was talking over her shoulder, and the man laughed at her remark. As they joined the small queue, the second woman peeled off and walked right up to me.

"Hello," she said, extending her hand, "I'm Violet."

I looked up in surprise; I had not realized at first that she wasn't with the couple she had walked in with. She was maybe a couple of years younger than I was, though I'm terrible at guessing ages. She was of medium height, and her eyes were a dazzling bright blue. She wore a completely white, ankle-length coat that she unbuttoned after shaking my hand, revealing a bright yellow cashmere sweater and equally bright yellow leather pants.

The most noticeable thing about her, however, was her hair. She wore it long and straight. And it was a deep burgundy red with streaks of bright cobalt blue.

"I'll be right back," she said, dropping her coat and a shoulder bag onto a chair at my table before joining the queue for a drink.

As she walked away, I remembered what had happened after Martin left my hotel room. Too embarrassed to stay when housekeeping arrived, I had grabbed the card from the windowsill and left to walk the streets of London for an hour while my room was transformed into a livable space again.

I had looked at the card again and again, trying to get a sense of who this Violet could be. The "she" that Martin had said would know what to do about my predicament. Whatever thoughts, images, and hopes my imagination had conjured, none of them were remotely close to the person I'd just met.

As Violet stood in the queue, her head moved constantly back and forth to take in the room. When she turned my way, she smiled quickly as her gaze met mine and then continued looking around her.

She was without a doubt the oddest dressed woman I had ever seen, and yet, there was an uncommon beauty to her. While her wardrobe was far brighter than any haute couture designer would approve of in February, it somehow made its own brazen, vibrant sense to me.

She came back with a drink and sat down in the chair opposite me. "You certainly aren't what I was expecting," she blurted. Her eyes met mine over the rim of her cup as she sipped her hot coffee before setting it down and looking around the room.

I mirrored her back-and-forth gaze, searching the small café for any sign of what she could be looking for. When my gaze returned to her, she was staring at me with a blank expression on her face. "I could say the same about you," I said. Then I added, "What were you expecting?"

She answered quickly, "Someone who looked like they'd been drinking solidly for the past five days and could barely stand."

I didn't miss a beat. "I've been sitting since you arrived."

Her head had continued moving from side to side, surveying the room again, even though only one new person had entered, and no one had left since she had sat down. When she heard my answer, a quick smile formed on her lips and just as quickly disappeared.

"Good point," she said as she refocused her wandering eyes on mine. She opened her mouth to say something but suddenly stopped, tilting her head slightly as a quizzical expression crossed her face. "What?"

"What?" I answered, confused.

"You're smiling."

"Umm," I said, suddenly nervous. "I . . . uh . . . don't know why I'm smiling." It was the truth.

"OK," she said. She took a quick sip of her drink. "Martin says you're running your company into the ground."

I inhaled a lungful of air quickly. I felt the urge to defend myself again, but I had thought a lot last night about how I was going to approach this meeting. I decided that whatever it was going to be about, and however Martin thought this woman could help me, I was going to simply listen without judgment.

It had sounded good last night, and on my walk to the café this morning, I had reminded myself that I had nothing to lose by listening and that I could decide on a course of action after the meeting was over.

That's fine from a theoretical standpoint. It's much harder to do when you're sitting face-to-face with someone who's blaming you for the state of your company's affairs, no matter how accurate that may be.

"Well," I began, "I'm not sure I would put it quite that way."

This time, she didn't hesitate. "How would you put it then?"

Her head remained on a constant swivel. She would look across the room to her left, look back at me, then look to her right before swinging her gaze back to me. Then she would begin the pattern again.

I knew her question should have unnerved me, but I felt oddly calm as I met her eyes. They were the brightest blue I had ever seen, and I wondered fleetingly if they were her actual color or contact lenses. She made eye contact for a moment before looking away as her revolving gaze continued.

"It's true," I said cautiously, "that we are struggling, but I don't know that it's accurate to say that I'm running it into the ground." I was careful to emphasize her own words as I repeated them back to her.

She brought her gaze back to me and leaned forward slightly, her arms resting on the table. "Is someone else running it into the ground?"

I smiled thinly and turned my head ever so slightly while still looking at her. "No," I replied slowly. I opened my mouth to continue, but she cut me off.

"But the company is pretty much collapsing, right?" she asked.

I stuttered a little as I answered, "Well . . . uhm . . . as I said, we are struggling right now . . ."

She didn't let me finish. "So," she said emphatically, "the company is being run into the ground and it's not someone else's doing, and you're the CEO . . . so . . . ?" As she finished, she raised her eyebrows questioningly.

"Look," I said, a touch defensive, "it's not that simple . . ." But she wouldn't let me continue.

"Yes, Ethan," she said plainly, "it is!"

Despite my resolution to listen, I couldn't help myself and opened my mouth to speak. Once again, she leaned forward even more. This time her eyes were sparkling with an intensity I couldn't escape. "I know all about what's been going on with your trip to London, your latest apps, and what you were hoping would be the breakthrough deal that would save the company."

She paused and sat up a little as she continued, "But that didn't work, and neither did your deal in Miami last month, or the one in Prague earlier this year."

How did she know about that? I had been discreet in my dealings in Prague, though clearly not discreet enough.

Violet, however, wasn't finished. "So, clearly the deals aren't working, which means the apps aren't going to be the magic savior." She paused and looked at me to make sure I was paying attention, then went on, "Sometimes, Ethan, as the saying goes, if you want to change some things in your life, you have to change some things in your life."

———— • ∞ • ————

Violet had known from an early age that her mind didn't work the way other people's minds worked. When she had been diagnosed as being on the spectrum, the uncle who had raised her (her parents having died when she was three) had sought the best doctors in the world to help them understand just what that meant.

There had been countless tests, drug therapy trials, fits of rage, shouting, throwing of plates or glasses or anything that came to hand. It had taken years to find the clinic in Switzerland that could help her understand her own place on the spectrum, and then months before they began making a dent in helping her manage it.

Her brain was simply wired differently. The "why" didn't matter to Violet. After all, there was nothing she could do about the reason she was the way she was.

What mattered, the only thing that mattered, was helping her control it.

She came to understand a great deal about how she was different through a lot of therapy and science—God, how she loved the science of it all. When she was ten years old, she began devouring information at a rate that would have alarmed most parents, but not Jeffery, whom she regarded as a surrogate father and mentor. He understood, even before she did, that she had capabilities beyond what even the doctors understood.

Most people's brains tend to focus on one thing at a time, with the subconscious taking on the more repetitive functions and tuning out the sensory input that isn't immediately required. As human beings learn how to multitask, they can focus on multiple things simultaneously, though it is not as effective as their singular focus.

Violet was never plagued with that dilemma. She always focused on everything, all at the same time, all the time. Most people wished they could have the aptitude and attention to detail that the famous Sherlock Holmes had, of being able to notice everything at a glance. Violet made the famous English detective seem rudimentary.

It was never about spotting criminals for her, however. Her brain simply took in everything and could process those inputs faster than neurotypical people's brains. She heard, smelled, and saw everything her senses could process at a speed that approached what might accurately be described as quantum-like.

The challenge for young Violet had been how to make sense of it all. So many doctors worked from the premise that they needed to help her focus on one thing at a time. After all, that's how most people function. So, they tried mood-altering drugs, trying to slow her brain down, which only frustrated her. Her brain, wired to take everything in, simply became sluggish and muddled.

Then Jeffery had posited a theory that led the team in Switzerland to completely change their approach. After so many attempts and failures, after watching his daughter struggle over the years, and perhaps simply because of his love for her and all the time spent holding her through her tears and fits of anger, he turned to the team of doctors and said:

"Maybe we're coming at this from the wrong end. I know we're trying to help her brain make sense out of all the 'data' she takes in, but it seems to me that we're forgetting one vital thing."

The team's lead doctor, a man by the name of Mathias, had kindly asked what he meant.

"Well," Jefferey had answered cautiously, "we're forgetting that her brain works much, much faster than ours. Maybe we don't need to slow her brain down but instead help it process at

its normal speed. Maybe this isn't a question of helping her focus but rather of how to prioritize. If her brain can handle taking everything in, surely it can handle sorting and prioritizing?"

The reaction wasn't immediate, but the team later acknowledged that this change of perception ultimately led them to find the "cocktail" of pharmaceuticals that now helped Violet lead a somewhat "normal" life.

There is always a trade-off when dealing with brain chemistry. Medical science just doesn't know enough, and Violet, despite all her research and deep dives into neuroscience, knew better than most that when you affect one thing, there is a corresponding effect somewhere else.

For Violet, her ability to read social cues was virtually nonexistent. Her brain, working at such a fast pace to process, tabulate, calculate, and filter all the data that was constantly coming in, left her just enough "processing" to be able to prioritize it all in a way that allowed her to communicate clearly. But "clearly" didn't mean "typically." She often spoke in short, to-the-point responses, unaware of the desire for more nuanced conversation from the people she was speaking with.

If asked, she could have instantly recounted what each person in the café was wearing, even those who had come and gone since her arrival. She knew many, if not all, of the orders that were placed (those she could hear over the noise) and even in what sequence. She knew how many tables and how many chairs the room contained, how many were currently occupied, and even which ones had wobbly legs.

If pressed, she could go to even more granular levels. She and Jeffery had played a game early on, when they were in a public place. He would ask her to look around and then close her eyes, and he would ask her random questions, sometimes to the most minute detail. Her recall was astonishing. It was more than mere photographic memory; it was like Google Earth where you could move around the scene, zoom in to a granular level, and see aspects you might not even notice the first time you looked at the image. But this volume of information coming at her made it difficult to have conversations about her. She was always focused on everything but herself.

For Violet, this happened every second of every day that she was awake. For the longest time, her medical team had struggled with the drain on her body, the toll that such an active mind took. While they were able to help her initially with handling the amount of data she took in, the drugs had a side effect of keeping her awake. She would go for days without sleep until her body collapsed from exhaustion.

Violet had been adamant that she did not want to take unnecessary medication, which meant she didn't want sleeping pills, the first course the team had recommended. She already felt she was meddling too much with her brain chemistry, and she simply didn't like the idea of adding to that just so she could sleep. She pushed back harder and harder, forcing them to find another solution.

Finally, after more than one near-tragic collapse that might have ended it all for her, they tried combining the drug cocktail they had formed with, of all things, homeopathic remedies that gave her body the ability to shut off each night. She could never get eight hours of sleep a night, but she could sleep, and that made all the difference.

Violet had met a great number of people in her life. She could remember all of them—well, almost all of them. She had only a few memories of her parents.

When her surrogate father had called to tell her the situation surrounding Ethan Knight, and to ask her to help as a favor to an old friend, she readily agreed. She had done her homework the night before, reading the various files her staff at the Life Prism Institute had sent her on Mr. Knight and his company.

She was being honest when she told him he wasn't what she expected as she sat down across the table from him. Her conversation with Martin Wesland last night on the phone had not painted a pretty picture. His description of the hotshot application developer—of not only his physical state but also his mental state—was one of a man at the end of his rope.

As she sat across from Ethan, telling him that if he wanted to change his life, he himself was going to have to change, she noticed for the second time in their conversation that a glimmer flashed behind his eyes. It wasn't a glimmer of anger, though perhaps that was hiding somewhere too. It was more a glimmer that some part of him—somewhere deep down, perhaps, but there nonetheless—still wanted to fight.

There was something, however, that bothered her.

Some people found her peculiar behavior unnerving; she understood that. Neurotypical people looked at one another as they talked. Perhaps one might look down at their drink or gaze briefly in the distance, but that was about the extent of it. Violet couldn't do that. Her brain's need for input would force her to scrutinize every facet of the person she was talking to; to the point that it would become uncomfortable, such was the intensity of her mind. This was one reason she was always looking around her environment when she was with someone. Partly because of her unquenchable need for data and simultaneously to not focus that intensity on the person she was with.

All of this was simply data her multifaceted brain would take in and file. What bothered her now, as she sat across from Ethan, was something unfamiliar. There was a presence about Ethan Knight that she couldn't figure out. Something in the way he looked at her. It was chemical, or at least that's what her brain was telling her. A reaction that went beyond normal conversation. Even more troubling was that when their eyes met, Violet felt something unfamiliar as well. A feeling she couldn't quite categorize.

Because of her overactive mind, Violet often regarded any external stimulus to her body, whether heat or cold, hunger, or even weariness, as simply more data to take in. Not something to focus on. Her brow wrinkled as she sat across from Ethan with these new sensations and thoughts flashing along the receptors of her brain. In mere microseconds, she evaluated everything she had seen, heard, and felt in the past few minutes, and suddenly she shifted from confused to a sense of wide-open clarity.

I'm attracted to him, *she thought with astonishment.*

"Excuse me," she said, and headed for the toilet. Once inside the small square room, she simply stood and looked in the mirror at her reflection while her brain worked on this new revelation.

Not that Violet had never found someone attractive before; she definitely had. Because of her unusual nature, she had been on very few dates, and none had gone well. Men just couldn't understand her or keep up with her. Violet had long ago given up any notions of romantic love and settled for her "world friends," as she called them. A small group of people across the globe that she'd managed to help in some fashion or another and who, although they too might not truly understand her, had become friends who appreciated her for who she was.

She stared at her reflection in the mirror. Not criticizing or primping but assessing. She was rapidly considering all her options, the ramifications, the pros and cons, the reality, likelihood, and percentage-based variations available to her in this situation.

Her conclusion was swift and precise. This was simply a chemical reaction between two people. Nothing more. Nothing less. She quickly and firmly suppressed her emotional reactions and refocused on the task at hand. If she was going to help Ethan Knight out of his current dire situation, there was no room for distraction for him or her.

She left the toilet and returned to the table, resolute in her decision.

Chapter 3
HABBIT21

I found myself staring at her as she turned her head to look around the room. She occasionally paused briefly as our eyes met. I watched as a crease appeared on her forehead beneath a strand of her burgundy-blue hair. There was something innocent and pure about the way her brow furrowed, and her head tilted slightly to one side. I could feel a smile cross my lips at the pleasure of watching her unemotional face suddenly transform and her eyes narrow as though some deep thought had crossed her mind.

Her eyes widened, and she stood up, excusing herself. I sat there with my coffee, oblivious to the customers coming and going, trying to make sense of it all.

She was peculiar in many ways, and I knew next to nothing about her, yet there was no denying that I had felt something when I looked into her eyes. Those eyes were mesmerizing, even if only for fleeting moments.

One thing was certain: I had no idea what was going on behind them. If she felt anything from our brief eye contact, I couldn't tell.

My rambling thoughts were pulled back to the present as she returned to the table. After sitting back down, she clasped her hands in front of her and looked straight across at me.

"After your early success," she began, "and after Martin helped you with your expansion, you went from impressive growth to a gradual decline that has now brought you to the point of impending collapse."

She said it plainly. A lawyer just laying out the facts.

I couldn't argue with her.

I noticed that her focus was entirely on me. She wasn't looking around the room. It made me a little nervous. "For the past eighteen months, you've been trying to find a way to save your company," she said.

I nodded.

"What about your staff?" she asked.

"My staff?" I replied, taken aback by the sudden question. "What about them?"

"Exactly."

I shook my head and leaned back in my chair, trying to understand what she was talking about. I lifted my hands, palms up. "I don't understand."

She looked at me for a few seconds with an odd expression I couldn't read. Then she blinked rapidly a few times and said, "Your early success was primarily due to your breakthrough application and working with your cofounders."

Again, I nodded.

"Once you expanded, however, you brought on some good people to help take on some of the load because you couldn't do it all by yourself."

"Yes, so?" I said defensively.

"So," she answered, "why are you still trying to do it all by yourself?"

I was getting a little tired of the veiled conversation. "Look," I said, "I'm not sure what you're trying to say, but why don't you just say it?"

"You still think the only way you can be successful is if you are the one who makes the company successful."

I stared at her blankly for a few seconds.

"Entrepreneurs believe that because they came up with an idea that they're the only ones who know what it takes to make things happen," she continued. "At first, that's OK, but once they see some modicum of success and their business grows, they make the fatal mistake of thinking that they are still the only ones that can make their enterprises continue to succeed."

"Hold on," I said. "I don't have some sort of ego complex. I hired great people because I knew I needed them to continue to be successful."

She nodded her head slightly, only now she was looking around the room again. I wondered fleetingly if she was still listening, but I pressed on anyway. "I don't think I'm the only one who can make my company successful, but I do think that it's up to me to make sure it is successful. Those employees depend on me." I emphasized the last point by jabbing myself in the chest with my index finger.

Her gaze swept back to me. "And how's that working out for you?"

My jaw dropped. I was about to respond when she said, "You are making two big mistakes. One, you think that because it's your company, and you started it, that everything is up to you, and you think you have all the answers. Two, you're focusing on the wrong thing."

"Oh really, the wrong thing," I said testily. "And what is that?"

"The same thing most companies focus on," she answered. "The bottom line."

I threw my hands up in exasperation. "The bottom line?" I said, perhaps a bit too loud. "Of course I'm worried about the bottom line, lady; I have to be. If I can't fix the bottom line, I'm out of business." Yep, I was definitely shouting now because people began to look over at our table, but I just glared back at them until they looked away.

The glances didn't seem to bother Violet at all. She looked at me and smiled. Her voice was even and calm as she said, "I agree. Fixing the bottom line needs to happen. What I said was that focusing on it is the wrong thing to do."

I was thinking that Martin had perhaps erred in thinking this woman would know how to help me, but I didn't have time to dwell on the thought.

"Fixating on the bottom line isn't going to help you," she said. "You need to focus on the bigger problem."

"What's a bigger problem than the fact that we're losing money?" I asked, trying to keep my voice even and losing the battle. I glanced again at a particularly nosy table with a glare I'm sure would have unnerved most people, but I didn't care anymore.

"Mismanagement," she said simply.

"Mis . . ." I began. "Wait . . . What?" I was completely at a loss for words.

She looked at her watch. "I can help you get your company back on track," she said. "But you're going to have to change a lot of things, starting with your belief that you're the only one with answers. What you've been doing hasn't been working, so, as far as I can see, you don't have too many options left."

With another quick glance around the café, she continued, "The biggest mistake companies make, big and small, is their inability to adapt to change. Sure," she said, "they will adapt to market changes, or adjust their service and product offerings, but they fail to change in the one area that can have the biggest impact."

"And what is that?" I asked, no longer hiding the sarcasm in my voice.

"The area that represents every company's greatest asset. The people."

Biting my tongue, I kept my mouth shut and listened.

"People," she continued, "are the lifeblood of every company and yet, by and large, the way most companies manage their people hasn't changed in decades."

Looking straight at me, she paused as our eyes made contact. Blinking a few times, she went on, "People, however, have changed. The workforce is changing, and the culture of what work means to people is changing. If you truly want to be successful and grow in this new age, you must change as well."

Violet began digging through her bag and pulled out an address book. An honest-to-goodness old-fashioned brown leather address book. "Normally I would have you work through this over the next several months, giving you time to implement the strategies and changes in between." She took a breath, scanned the room quickly from left to right, then focused back on me with a look that left no doubt of her conviction. "But we don't have that kind of time."

I couldn't agree more. In a few months, never mind several, my company was going to come to a crashing halt. Sure, I could throw more of my own money at it, but I would only be throwing it away; good money after bad, as they say. No, I'd realized over a year ago that my company's days were numbered. I just really thought I would have figured out a way forward by now. Months were not the kind of time I had. On that, Violet and I were in complete agreement.

Once again, her voice brought me back from my meandering thoughts. "So, we're going to take the crash course and do it in one month."

I raised my eyebrows at that one. I still had no idea what she was talking about, but it seemed unlikely that the kind of systemic change she was alluding to would be effective after just one month. Not, as she had clearly pointed out, that I had a lot of other choices.

As if reading my mind, she added, "It's not a lot of time, and you're not going to be out of the woods in four weeks. You're going to have to do a lot of work during this next month, and then we'll see."

"What does that mean?"

Violet didn't seem to hear my question. She continued looking at the people standing in line and sitting all around us. "Normally, this is something we would work on for the better part of a year. I've never actually tried to do it this quickly before, and whether it is successful will come down to . . ." She paused as she brought her gaze back, and once again her beautiful blue eyes bored directly into mine. "Put it this way. Once you do the work over the next four weeks, whether it ultimately succeeds won't be up to you at all."

I was more confused than ever.

Violet pulled out her phone and, consulting her address book, punched in a phone number. Then she stood and walked toward the front door of the café. I heard her say, "Hi, it's Violet," before going outside as an incoming customer held the door for her.

Why, I wondered, didn't she just use the contacts on her phone instead of using an address book? I watched as she paced back and forth in front of the large window, talking and smiling into the phone for a few minutes, before she switched off and came back inside.

"I want you to meet someone before you leave England." Reaching into her bag, she pulled out a notebook and turned to a blank page. She wrote something down, tore off the page, and passed it across the table to me. "She's expecting you tomorrow morning at nine."

I looked down at the name on the page. It read Felicity Taylor with an address. The name meant nothing to me.

"I'll call you tomorrow afternoon, and we can discuss next week." She stood up, grabbed her bag, and stuck out her hand.

"I, umm." I stumbled to my feet and took her hand. "Hold on," I said, dumbfounded, and looked down at the sheet of paper she'd handed me. "Who is this person and why should I change my plans to meet her?"

Violet simply turned and started walking out of the café. I grabbed my coat and scrambled after her, nearly careening into a mom taking her baby out of its pram.

"Would you wait a minute?" I said, catching up to her. "At least tell me what this whole four-week thing is you're talking about."

She glanced over at me, almost surprised to see me there. She said, "I've developed a program I call HABBIT21."

"Don't tell me," I said. "It has twenty-one habits for successful management?" As before, I didn't try to hide the sarcasm and even threw in an eye roll for good measure.

Again, the sarcasm didn't seem to register with her. She simply said, "No, it's an acronym, spelled H-A-B-B-I-T twenty-one."

I groaned out loud. "Great," I said, stretching the word as though it almost had two syllables. "Just what I need, another business leadership acronym."

Violet turned her head, but this time I cut her off. "Look, no offense," I said, "but every guru and so-called expert has an acronym. Go to any bookstore in any airport in the world and there's a table ladened down with books, and all of them have the magic acronym to help you succeed."

"Don't worry, it doesn't mean there are twenty-one habits. It stands for the 'Humanagement Approach to Better Business In The 21st century.'"

I blinked several times, still not sure what she was talking about. "Ummm," I said stupidly, "what is the . . . um . . . Humanagement approach. . . ?" I had already forgotten the rest.

"It consists of a multi-disciplinary approach to human management," she said matter-of-factly, "versus the traditional approach which focuses on outcomes, driven by revenue, rather than people."

I wanted to ask exactly what she meant by that, but she had more to say.

"It means," she said, stopping and turning toward me, "that even if you do the work, if you buy into the HABBIT21 program lock, stock, and barrel, it remains to be seen if things can turn around before . . . well, before it all comes crashing down."

"Gee," I said sarcastically, "that sounds inspiring."

"Don't be late tomorrow," she responded, and turned to walk away. I stood there speechless, holding the paper in my hand, and watched her go.

Violet walked away and turned in the direction of her tube station. Her head, ever on its constant swivel, took in the sights and smells and sounds around her as she walked.

Despite the multitude of sensations London offered her, however, her focus was still in the café. She was replaying every facet of the conversation in her mind. She had smiled when she saw Ethan get defensive. There was fight left in him yet, she had thought. His ego was much smaller than most CEOs she knew, though still present. His sense of responsibility, though misguided, was honorable. There was no question he was bright, and his skill and intelligence had gotten him this far. He had a long way to go, however, if he was going to save his company and help the employees he clearly cared for. If she could get him to understand where he was going wrong, that was the key.

Entrepreneurs were a special breed, and this one might prove to be her biggest challenge to date. The thought didn't scare Violet or cause her angst. It was one of many thoughts flying through her mind as she passed among the throng of humanity on the London sidewalk.

She shook her head, trying to clear some room in her stream of thoughts.

A vendor was calling out his wares on her left as she turned to cross the street. As she waited for the light to change, she watched a double-decker bus pass by, full of commuters and tourists traversing the crowded streets of England's largest city. Across the street, a mother was scolding a crying child whose hand she was holding. An older couple was walking arm in arm; the gentleman, his body succumbing to age, now relied on his wife for support. Several people around her were looking at their phones, texting, or talking into earpieces. She took it all in.

This was her life. People. Watching them, cataloging them, researching them, helping them.

People like Ethan Knight, she thought to herself, and smiled.

Chapter 4
Felicity

I returned to the hotel and, despite it still being early in the morning, my body was still reeling, and what I really wanted to do was crawl back into bed and go to sleep. Instead, I took a long, hot bath and drank some sweet English tea. I'd heard somewhere that sweet tea was good for you if you weren't feeling well, and I was the personification of understatement where that was concerned.

I got out of the bath and, with a towel draped around my waist, picked up the piece of paper Violet had given me. Perhaps I should Google this Felicity Taylor. Find out who she was, what she did, get a leg up on this meeting I was going to have with her tomorrow.

The truth is I was too tired. Or maybe I had stopped caring altogether. Whatever was going to happen tomorrow, I was just going to let it happen. I was tired of fighting, tired of trying to figure everything out. I was well and truly resigned to whatever fate had in store for me.

Looking back, it was this complete and utter apathy about what was going to happen next that would end up helping me the most.

***

The next morning, I was as surprised as anyone to find myself in a suit and tie, waiting in the lobby of a well-appointed office suite in a prestigious part of London's business district. I had arrived promptly at 9:00 a.m. for my meeting with Felicity Taylor. After I announced myself, the receptionist asked me to take a seat and inquired if I wanted a cup of tea, coffee, or water while I waited.

I'm not sure she would have had time to make tea had I said yes, because no sooner did I sit down than a woman in her late forties or early fifties approached me with her hand outstretched. "Hello," she said, "I'm Felicity. You must be Ethan."

I stood back up and shook her hand. She wore gray pants with a cream-colored blouse that suited her black hair and gray eyes and accentuated her dark brown skin. Her handshake was firm and yet soft at the same time. She smiled warmly and invited me back to her office.

I had at least Googled her on the cab ride over and knew she was the CEO of an accounting firm. Although I expected the traditional corner office with a view of the city, she led me instead to an office in the middle of a long hallway. Although it was bigger than the one next to it, it was the same as any other office we had passed.

We sat at a small round table in front of her desk. Behind the desk was a large plate-glass window with a sweeping view overlooking the sprawling business district of London. Though this was not the tallest building, we were high enough to see for miles.

Felicity asked me how I knew Violet.

"I don't really," I said. "I just met her this week." I didn't want to sound crazy by saying I'd only met her yesterday and was blindly following her recommendation knowing nothing about why I was doing this, or even what I was doing. "She was recommended by a friend," I added by way of explanation, then said, "What about you?"

A large smile appeared on Felicity's face, and she tilted her head to one side as though remembering something fondly. "Oh," she said almost wistfully, "a friend introduced us as well." Then she looked at me, still smiling, and said, "Although I feel like I've known her for ages now." She paused, then added, "So, Violet wants me to introduce you to Humanagement."

I was used to executives getting right down to business but wasn't sure how to respond. "I suppose so," I said tentatively. "To be honest, I'm not sure what this is all about."

"Well," Felicity began, "Humanagement is a concept Violet constructed based on the changes in work culture, technology, and the employee–company dynamics that we face in our modern working world. Tell me, have you ever had any management training?"

"Not really," I answered. "I mean, I've read a few books or whatever, but mostly I just figured it out as I went along."

"That's typical, I'm afraid," Felicity proclaimed, "though even if you had taken courses, you'd like as not have learned how to manage the same way people have been managing for centuries." Her accent was typically London-sounding, and she talked in that clear, crisp way most Londoners do, enunciating every word.

"Is there something wrong with the way people have been managing?"

"Oh yes!" she replied, her voice rising sharply. "There most definitely is. You see, Ethan, times have changed.

Companies have had to adapt to the way they do business. Technology has changed." Then she paused ever so slightly before she added, "People have changed."

I wasn't sure what to say to that, so I just kept listening.

"Violet came up with Humanagement because she felt, and I agree with her, that companies have for far too long focused on one thing and one thing only." She paused for effect. "The bottom line. Don't get me wrong," she said quickly, holding up one hand and probably sensing my eye roll beginning to develop. "We all have to pay attention to the bottom line. It's just that focusing on that and that alone is not how we become successful."

"Tell that to my accountant," I said.

Felicity laughed and nodded, then said, "We are an accounting firm. Business has been focusing so much on the bottom line that we've lost sight of what our greatest assets are, our one sure way of ensuring that our companies succeed." She paused, wanting to make sure I understood and listened to her next point carefully. "Ethan, the one thing we should be focusing on, and the one thing we've put at the bottom of our priority lists for too long, is our people."

Leaning forward a little, she said, "The Humanagement Pillars that Violet taught me are exactly what they sound like: human management. The management of people. When we focus on helping our people 'be and become' the best people they can be, the byproduct of that is increased teamwork, increased quality, increased production. In short, increased success, and what does that equate to?" She raised one eyebrow dramatically. "Increased revenue and ultimately, an increased bottom line."

After a pause, she continued, "You see, we've been going at it all wrong. We thought if we scrimped and saved, cut costs here, downsized there, always focusing on the bottom line, that we could save and efficiencize our way to success." She laughed a warm laugh and added, "I'm not sure 'efficiencize' is actually a word, but it fits."

I laughed with her and said, "OK, I think I understand what you mean, but are you saying that downsizing or finding efficiencies is a bad thing?"

"No, not at all," she answered. "At least, not some of the time. What I'm saying is simply that we've always focused on the result, and we stopped paying attention to how we get that result. The Pillars of Humanagement are a way of refocusing on what's important. By shifting our focus onto what really matters in our company, the people, we have completely transformed what we do, how we do it, and who we are as a company. The results," she concluded, "have been beyond anything I could have imagined."

"Sounds almost too good to be true."

"Well," she said, "all I can tell you is that they work for me, and for many other people Violet has helped. I am an enthusiastic believer in Violet and her work."

I wasn't sure what to think, but I'd come this far, and besides, I was out of options. "OK, so how does this Humanagement thing work?"

"Violet gave me a quick synopsis of your accelerated time-line and asked me to give you the first three Pillars because they sort of go together. The first Pillar of Humanagement is Hiring," she said plainly. "Now tell me, how do you go about hiring someone?"

"Well, uhm . . ." I stammered, not ready for the question. ". . . I mean, you know, we have them fill out an application, go through interviews—pretty typical, I guess."

Felicity seemed genuinely interested and began asking questions. "Who makes the final decision?"

"It depends on the department," I said. "I usually do on developers because that's my background, but I let our CFO hire his staff, and sales is handled by the department head."

She nodded as I talked. "And do you have any tests for who gets hired and who doesn't?"

"You mean like some of those IQ or personality tests?" I asked.

Felicity nodded.

"I looked into some," I said. "I saw a presentation at a conference on one, too. It was interesting, but it was a lot of money and took a lot of time, and we just aren't that big of an organization. I didn't think it would be worth it."

"I understand," she said. "I certainly see why a lot of companies use those tests. They're trying to find people who 'fit' into their organizations." She emphasized the word "fit" with air quotes.

"It makes sense," she continued. "We all want good people, on good teams, working together and being as productive as they can be. The problem is that most companies make hiring such a black-and-white process that they forget we're dealing with human beings, and human beings don't all do things the same way."

Felicity sat back in her seat and looked across the table at me. "The first and most important component of the first Pillar of Humanagement, or Hiring, is to always hire people smarter than you." She raised her voice at the word "smarter" and emphatically pronounced it. "The biggest mistake managers make when they become the head of a company is thinking that they must have all the answers and therefore must be the smartest person in the room. The reality is, Ethan, you need to be the dumbest person in the room."

I raised my eyebrows at that one, but she held up her hand to keep me from talking and said, "No, I'm not saying CEOs should be stupid."

We both smiled at that remark.

"What I am saying is that you are hiring someone to do a job at your company. A job you can't do because you are the CEO and have other responsibilities. So, when you hire that person, you'd better make sure they are the best person for the job. Which means they should be better at that job than you. Besides," she went on, "not only would it be impossible for you to do every job in a company as CEO, but even if you could, you wouldn't be able to keep up with new advances, new technologies, new ways of doing those jobs. So, hire someone who can, and make sure they're the best you can get."

I pursed my lips as I mulled over what she was saying. I'd always hired good people, but now I was thinking about it differently. Had I always made sure the people I hired were better than me? Certainly, in sales and finance, areas I knew little about, chances were that the lowest-level employee knew more than I did, but when it came to software developers and IT, I wasn't so sure I could say the same thing.

Felicity interrupted my thoughts. "The next piece of this Pillar is the CV. You call them résumés in America, I believe. We have for so long put so much emphasis on CVs that now there are people giving classes on how to create one that will make an employee stand out and get that coveted job."

I nodded. I'd also seen advertisements online for courses like that over the years.

"I don't care much for CVs," Felicity said.

Again, my eyebrows rose, but Felicity kept going before I could say something. "CVs are merely a calling card. They give you a little information, but their primary purpose is to determine eligibility. Yes, I know some people can be really creative, and it's fun to see when it happens, but so little of what you are looking for can be determined by a creative or unique CV. It becomes too easy to build a picture in your mind before you even meet someone, and that can have a disastrous effect if you don't keep it in check."

"So," I said quickly, wanting to get my question in before she continued, "you're saying it really doesn't matter what someone has on their res . . . I mean CV?"

"It only matters from the standpoint that they have some of the qualifications you're looking for in that position," she answered. "Of course, it's nice if they include a personal cover letter, and yes, it's good if they don't make silly grammatical errors or forget to change the name of the last company they sent the same CV to. I would argue that we've all made mistakes and that shouldn't be the only reason you reject someone. Regardless, I coach my people to simply look at the facts on the CV. Does this person qualify for the type of job we're hiring for? That doesn't mean that they fit every criterion, by the way," she said, "but I'll get to that soon. If they qualify, they move on to step two."

"Step two being an interview."

"Step two being a phone interview," Felicity corrected. "This is where you can get a sense of the person. Most of the conversation is simply getting a little more information on their history and work background from the CV. The phone interview helps you narrow down your pool from the CVs. What is their personality like on the phone? Are they likable? Do they seem confident in their answers? How well do they communicate? One thing I tell my team is to remember that this is how our clients and customers will likely have their first interaction with our company. Do you like what you hear? Do you like the person you're talking to? If you were a customer, what would your perception of our organization be after talking to this person?"

I felt like I should be taking notes, but I hadn't brought any paper with me, and as crazy as it sounds for an app developer, I really don't like taking notes on my phone.

"When you're the CEO of a rather large company like mine, it's impossible to be involved in every hiring decision.

So, you create a culture where all your managers hire the same way. It takes effort, and it takes time. It takes a commitment to hiring the right people for the right job." She pointed her finger at me as she said those words.

"When you can," she continued, "you want to sit down with the final candidate before they're hired. Obviously, if you're hiring an executive, you'll do this anyway, but I always try to keep my hand in from time to time, and not just with department heads or leadership team hires. Sometimes I'll ask to see the final candidate for an entry-level position."

"Really?" I asked, surprised. "Why?"

"Because this is my company," Felicity answered, "and I want to make sure we're hiring the right people whether at the bottom, the middle, or the top." She paused before adding, "When I interview someone, I don't have set questions, or trick questions. I don't ask what they're best at or what their biggest weakness is or any of those tried-and-true standards of interviewing."

I leaned forward in my chair. "So, what do you ask them?"

Felicity smiled and said, "I tell them right away that I won't be asking any of those things I just mentioned. I tell them I want to have a conversation with them, no specific questions, no hidden agendas. I tell them I want to get to know them, and I want them to get to know me and my company. After all, I tell them, being a good fit isn't just a one-way street. I know they want the job, and if they've come this far, they're qualified to do the job. My purpose in meeting them is to see if I can determine if they're a good fit in the company and if the company is a good fit for them."

"So, what do you talk about?"

"Oh, it all depends," she said. "We just start talking and I'll ask questions based on what they say about themselves.

I'll also ask what they want out of a company they're going to exchange their precious time to work for."

"OK," I said slowly. "So how do you know if they're a good fit or not and vice versa?"

"You can usually tell," Felicity said, and with a soft expression she added, "It's going to sound strange, but you have to trust your instincts. You'll know. You sort of just get a feeling about whether it's a good fit either way."

I thought about this for a moment. Then I asked her, "And have you ever gone back to the hiring manager and told them you didn't think it was a good fit? Or have you yourself ever regretted hiring someone you thought was a good fit?"

Felicity laughed good-naturedly. "Oh yes," she said. "But not at first. At first, I didn't trust my instincts, and I didn't want to make waves or hurt a manager's feelings, and I certainly didn't want to admit I was wrong." She paused and looked at me, no doubt reading my expression and knowing that was exactly what I had been thinking. "After I allowed one of my managers to hire someone I didn't feel good about and it caused havoc in the department, I said never again. Same when it was my own fault. It's not always easy, but I've found that if you continue to empower your people by explaining to them what you're thinking, they're often quite amenable.

"Now," she said. "Let's move on to the second Pillar."

Chapter 5
The Second Pillar

I watched as Felicity's eyes gleamed. "Would it surprise you to know that we don't have a human resources employee on staff?"

"Yes, actually," I answered

"We contract out with a small firm that handles some of those functions for us, benefits and such, but we have taken on many of the traditional functions within our daily operations, and we simply don't need someone dedicated to it full time."

Felicity sat back in her chair and crossed her legs. "One thing we've been able to get rid of is annual performance appraisals."

She must have seen the surprise on my face because she beamed at me.

"What do you mean you've gotten rid of them?"

"We don't have them."

"What?" I asked. "None at all?"

"Not in the traditional sense, no. That's the second Pillar of Humanagement." Felicity stood up and walked over to the window overlooking the bustling city. Turning back to me, she said, "Do you know what the number one reason employees leave a company is?"

I thought about it for a moment and then said, "Probably money."

"Compensation is what most people think," she answered, "but in fact it's not the primary reason." She paused for a beat. "The number one reason most people leave their employment is that they don't feel appreciated or valued."

I shrugged. "Surely that's tied into money though, isn't it?"

"Everyone wants to be paid more," she said, "but you can pay someone a great deal of money and if they feel they aren't appreciated for their work, they'll still leave. It's true that for some people their value is tied to how much they are paid, but it isn't the only measure, whether or not they realize it."

I took in that last statement and thought about whether it resonated with me, but she wasn't finished.

"Employees, like all human beings, need to feel as though what they do matters. They want to know they're making a difference, even if that difference is only in their department or just within their role in the company." Returning to the table, she continued, "Most research will tell you it is because of dissatisfaction with their immediate supervisor that employees leave, but Violet wanted to know more, so she delved into it. She found the root cause, regardless of who is responsible for it, is that people simply want to know that they matter.

"The biggest reason employees feel underappreciated or that their work has little to no value is more often than not attributed to lack of communication, or perhaps better put, lack of appropriate communication, with their supervisors." She took a deep breath and continued, "You see, Ethan, most supervisors don't talk with their employees; they talk *to* them."

She let that sink in and then said, "Typically, the only time they talk about how the employee is doing is at that annual performance appraisal, and even then, it's usually to admonish them for things they haven't done, or at best, to regurgitate what the employee has written in their own self-appraisal." At this, Felicity made a face as though she had just opened a bottle of spoiled milk and sniffed the contents.

"Now," she said, "we've already talked about hiring the right people for the right job, so hopefully, we're starting with supervisors who have been learning about and believe in Humanagement. So, we can dispense with how *not* to do things. The second Pillar of Humanagement is to practice IPF and HICCUPs."

She must have seen the blank look on my face, but she simply smiled and continued.

"IPF stands for Immediate Performance Feedback. We don't need annual performance appraisals because we do them in real time, all the time. Whether an employee has done something good or bad, we give them immediate feedback. The key here is to praise publicly and admonish privately." She said the last part slowly, emphasizing her point. "There is *never* a good reason to point out someone's error or fault in front of their peers. No good can come of it."

That made sense to me, but I was also curious about something. "So, I imagine your managers and supervisors must spend a lot of time talking to their employees about what they're doing well and what they need to do better. When do they have time to do their own work?"

Felicity smiled a knowing smile like I had just walked into a trap. "The answer to the first part is both yes and no, but before I explain, let me just say that the reason you think that way is because you are thinking the way most people do about the function of management. The truth is that the primary function of managers and supervisors *is* to talk to their employees. That 'other' work you're talking about should be a minor part of their tasks." Now it was her turn to raise her eyebrows at me, as if challenging me to dispute what she had just said.

Stepping into one trap was bad enough, so I kept my mouth shut, though she could clearly see from my expression that I had doubts about what she was saying.

She nodded briefly. "So, if the first part is to provide immediate feedback when appropriate, the second part, HICCUP, stands for Human Interactive Conversations and Constant Updating Principle."

It was certainly a mouthful, and as I processed the words of the acronym, Felicity went on to explain what they meant. "The Human Interactive Conversations part deals with talking to your employees *in person*," she said, emphasizing the last two words. "It's so easy with technology to send an instant message or a text or an email, but those are too impersonal, too often subject to misinterpretation or even laced with sarcasm that may or may not be received the same way the sender intended."

I had to agree with her there, as I had often had my own sarcasm fall on deaf ears, so to speak, when sent electronically.

"The emphasis here," she said, "is to talk to employees face-to-face. It doesn't always have to be at their desk or in the supervisor's office, either. We encourage our supervisors to take employees for walks, get them coffee or lunch—anything to get them away from the distractions of their jobs. The idea is to talk with them, and that's not always easy to do in the office, where people are vying for attention, phones are buzzing or ringing, and emails are flooding in.

"The second part of HICCUP is the Constant Updating Principle, which doesn't quite explain the concept fully because it's really a two-way street."

I tilted my head to one side, not quite understanding.

"Part of the reason for these conversations is to update the employee on their purpose, their value, their piece of the puzzle in the organization," Felicity went on. "For example, if we're planning a major change in the organization, rather than have a department-wide meeting and explaining the coming change, supervisors meet one-on-one with employees to explain not only the change but how that employee will be affected and how they will affect the change."

I had to interrupt her. "But wouldn't that take forever in a large department or company like yours?"

"You would think so, but it actually doesn't," she answered quickly. "You certainly use the trickle-down effect of having department heads talk to their managers, who in turn talk to their supervisors, who then talk to their employees, and that helps."

"Yes," I said, wanting to push the point, "but don't you then run into a game of telephone where what the department head told their manager ends up differing from what gets relayed to the employees?"

Again, Felicity smiled. "Not if it's done correctly and you have a culture of transparency." Seeing my frown, she said, "That game of telephone, where information gets changed and distorted, often happens because people are holding back, hiding information, wanting to 'protect' their employees from something. But when you're honest, open, and transparent, there's no reason to change the message."

I considered that as she paused, trying to wrap my head around the validity of it, but she still wasn't finished.

"Also, that department head doesn't really know exactly how the change will affect each employee, but their immediate supervisor does, so it only makes sense they should be the one having that direct conversation."

I nodded slowly as it made more sense.

"There's the other side of that two-way street though," she said, "and that is that the CUP part of HICCUP has to do with getting to know, and staying up to date, with each employee and what is going on in their lives, both professionally and personally. This goes back to the 'human being' part of our employees," she explained. "We were all taught not to bring our personal lives or problems into work, but that's impossible. What happens to us outside of work is bound to affect us *at* work."

Felicity leaned forward and looked at me to make sure she had my attention. "The problem occurs when we as managers *don't* know what's going on outside of work. Can you imagine being frustrated with an employee who seems distracted and unable to pay attention, who is not following through in their day-to-day work, misses deadlines, et cetera? You'd probably be ready to reprimand or even fire them, and if you were on the annual performance appraisal schedule, you might not even wait until then to do it."

She raised her arms, palms up, as if to say, "Right?"

I shrugged and nodded.

"So, what would you do if you found out that the reason for your employee's behavior was that they had just found out their spouse had been diagnosed with cancer?" She raised her eyebrows again, then added, "It changes your perspective on their behavior, doesn't it?"

I had to admit she was right.

"So, you see, it's important that we understand not only what makes our employees tick and how they work but also what's going on with them. I don't mean that you have to be best friends with everyone who works for you, but you have to establish a relationship with them, a rapport that allows them to feel comfortable enough to come and talk to you about what's going on, whether or not it's at work.

"You'll learn more about this in the fourth Pillar of Humanagement, but the point is that if we communicate on a regular basis, if we practice IPF and HICCUPs year-round, there's no need for performance appraisals because we're reviewing, adjusting, and providing feedback constantly."

I began to see the merit of what she was saying. "I suppose making adjustments year-round makes more sense than once a year," I said, nodding slowly.

"It's a lot like sailing," she responded, which took me by surprise. "Imagine if you only checked your course once a week on a boating trip around the world. Far better to constantly check your course, and correct daily, if you want to make your trip a success.

"Oh, and one more thing. This method gets rid of the often-used, much-maligned concept of the employee self-appraisal." Again, she made the sour milk face. "I've always hated that concept because it always felt to me like I was writing my own performance appraisal and doing my bosses' jobs for them. What a waste of time, if you ask me."

A thought occurred to me. "Wait a minute. If you don't have annual appraisals, how do you deal with raises?"

"Good question," she said, "and it has a simple answer. We determine raises on each employee's anniversary date. No big review of performance, no big meeting. Just another normal conversation between employee and supervisor like they've been having all year round, only this time we talk about money."

Lifting her index finger in the air, she said, "And this is one of the most important points. When IPF and HICCUP are done correctly, there are no surprises come raise time. And if there *is* a surprise, then we know communication hasn't been successful and that's where the problem lies.

Ultimately, if you've been open and honest with each other and there's transparent communication year-round, no one is surprised at the amount of the raise, or lack thereof."

Felicity sat up straight and took a deep breath. "Which leads us to the third, and perhaps most difficult, Pillar."

I waited eagerly to hear what it was.

"Firing."

Chapter 6
The Third Pillar

Urgh . . . I had to agree that firing was one of the least, if not *the* least attractive things about being a boss.

Felicity dove right in. "I don't know of a single CEO, department head, or manager that enjoys sacking"—she caught herself—"firing people, and if they did, they wouldn't be working for me."

I smiled ruefully.

"There simply is no 'easy' way to fire someone." She used air quotes for emphasis. "The goal, of course, is to communicate so well that even firing someone doesn't come as a surprise, but even with the best use of IPF and HICCUPs, there are some people who just don't see it coming."

She looked away from me briefly and I thought I saw something sad fleetingly cross her face. Turning her gaze back to me, she smiled and continued, "As with all things, Violet has figured out the best way to do this too. When you fire someone, do it quickly. Pull the plaster—I think you call them Band-Aids—right off." She mimicked pulling one off her arm quickly. "Don't sugarcoat or reason away what's about to happen. Get the elephant out of the room and tell them straightaway."

I nodded my understanding, remembering my own awkward attempts at easing into telling someone I was letting them go. It never helped.

"Again," she said, "if you've done the first two Pillars correctly, this shouldn't come as a complete surprise, though to some, it will. Human nature, however, rarely lets people take a blow like this quietly. They will want to know why; they will want to argue and defend their actions. Don't fall into that trap. Nothing they can say is going to change your mind, and nothing you can say is going to convince someone who doesn't think they deserve to be sacked to suddenly agree with you." Felicity pitched her voice higher, mimicking someone else as she said, "Oh, of course, I see it now. That makes perfect sense. Absolutely, I must go."

We both smiled at the absurdity of it.

"And conversely, you're not going to say"—this time she lowered her voice as low as it could likely go—"Oh yes, I understand now, never mind, we're not going to sack you, you can go back to your desk now."

Again, we both smiled.

"There's just no point in arguing or reasoning when you've come to this point. The important thing is to stick to the facts. Don't get emotionally charged. Don't try to overexplain why or what or when. Just state the facts."

After a pause, she said, "This doesn't mean, however"— her tone softened again as she leaned forward—"that you must be cold, heartless, or cruel. In fact, it means just the opposite. You should be kind."

I really should have brought some paper to take notes with, I thought for the second time.

"You are changing their world as they know it. Changing jobs, especially when it is not your choice, is one of the most life-altering events we can go through. Try to put yourself in their shoes and remember that this is far more difficult for them to hear than it is for you to tell them, and that's saying something."

I smiled a thin smile again, knowing exactly what she meant. Firing, to me, had always been a painful and difficult thing to do.

"Above all else, be kind. Firm in your resolve, but kind in your interaction."

I had the impression that this was something she had said before, or more likely, was something she said often to her own managers.

"This is perhaps the most important time to live the Golden Rule," she said. "Treat them the way you would like to be treated if it were happening to you."

I sat for a minute, taking in all she had told me.

"What if," I began, "you have to let people go because of downsizing?"

"Ahhh," she replied. "Again, it all goes back to IPF and HICCUPs, doesn't it? If you've been open and honest with them as a company, then downsizing won't come as a complete shock to anyone. None of us may like it, but at least it won't be something they haven't thought about."

She checked her watch. "Which leads me to one quick point, though technically I'm getting ahead of things and into future Pillars."

I was leaning forward now, eager to hear what she was about to say, like a child in school when the teacher says she's going to tell them a secret.

"If you do find yourself letting people go for economic or other downsizing reasons, you should do everything you can to help them find employment before you let them go."

Standing up, she glanced at her watch again and said, "I think we've covered quite enough today, don't you?"

Taking my cue, I too stood up and thanked her for spending so much time with me.

"It's rather a crash course, I'm afraid. There's really a lot more to it, but as I understand from Violet, time is not something you have much of."

I nodded in response to her raised eyebrows. "Yes, that's very true, I'm afraid."

"Well," she said as she walked me down the hall and back to the main entrance, "you're in good hands with Violet." Taking my hand to shake farewell, she added, "If anyone can help you, it's her."

Just like that, I found myself out on the street, looking up at the gray clouds and the promise of rain. I wondered if Violet and her Pillars of Humanagement could indeed help me or if, like the drizzle that began to fall from the dark clouds above, it was already too late.

———— • ⧯ • ————

Violet was at that very moment hurtling beneath the streets of London on the Piccadilly line with her noise-canceling earbuds firmly in place and Vivaldi's Four Seasons Spring blasting. She felt her phone vibrate and took it out of her coat pocket. There was a text message from Felicity.

She responded with a brief thank-you and several emojis, with more hearts of varying colors than were perhaps appropriate.

Felicity's response was quick: my pleasure. any time. coffee soon? *followed by more than one line of hearts.*

Violet wondered how Ethan had received the first three Pillars. Felicity's text said it had gone well, and that she had tried to focus on the main points, as she and Violet had discussed.

Felicity said that he had asked good questions and had been appropriately skeptical, as well as appropriately impressed.

So far so good, Violet thought. Felicity had stated the obvious in closing out her initial text: **What he will or can do with it is anyone's guess. You've really taken on quite the project, haven't you?**

That was the real question, wasn't it? Make that questions, emphasis on the plural, she thought. Could the app wizard change himself in such a short period of time? Would he be able to institute such large-scale changes in his company so quickly? And most of all, would it be enough?

Violet pondered these questions, all the while looking up and down the carriage, noticing detail after detail of her surroundings and the sea of humanity that rocked back and forth as the train careened steadily to the next stop. Simultaneously, her mind fell into synchronous time with Vivaldi's beautiful violins as the orchestra in her earphones ebbed and flowed with the music of the seasons and the train swayed back and forth.

Despite all this activity, and the tasks it kept her mind busy with, she still pondered the mystery that had begun at the café the day before. What was it that nagged at her about Ethan Knight? What had she missed? She'd spent a good portion of the previous night going through new material her staff had garnered on his company and his rise to Silicon Valley stardom, as well as the original information they had sent her the day before.

She knew as much about Mr. Knight and his business as there was to know without being an insider in the company itself. Still, her mind was unsettled. There was something else, she was sure of it. Just what "it" was remained a mystery. She knew she'd have to be patient until she could learn more.

Patience did not come easily for Violet.

Her fingers moved across the virtual keys on her screen faster than most people can type on an actual keyboard. Heard things went well with Felicity. Will meet you in St. Louis a week from tomorrow. Get to work. She signed the text "**V.**"

Chapter 7
Sam

I stared at the screen. *St. Louis? In a week?* I wanted to laugh, but then she had said this was going to be a crash course condensed down to a month. What exactly did I expect? Of course, I had more questions than answers at this point.

I hit reply and typed my response: "*Yes, Felicity was . . . interesting. St. Louis? Care to give me a little insight?*"

Her response came back faster than I would have thought possible. "*More info to come on St. Louis. Focus on the first 3 Pillars for now. You have 7 days to implement them.*"

I had to reread her message twice to make sure I hadn't misunderstood. She expected me to implement the first three Pillars in seven days. Did she not realize that those seven days included the weekend, when most of my company would not be working? That changing culture and processes take time? I shook my head, bewildered.

I was in a cab heading back to my hotel, and I must have grumbled some of my thoughts out loud because the cab driver looked in his rearview mirror and said, "Sorry, what was that, sir?"

"Just thinking out loud." I tried to ignore his raised eyebrows and disbelieving expression as we wove our way through London's busy center toward the hotel.

I realized that if I was going to have any hope of making changes of any kind, I couldn't wait for the flight I was now booked on for tomorrow. I emailed Sam, my assistant, to get me the earliest possible booking today, which is how, three hours later, I was rushing through Heathrow Airport to catch my flight for the long ride home.

Just before I boarded, I received an email from the Life Prism Institute. The subject of it read "On behalf of Violet," and it included several documents on the first three Pillars of HABBIT21. I spent the better part of the first half of the flight going through them and making notes on how to approach things once I was back in the office.

I woke up just as we were landing and exited the plane. Having flown overnight, I was jet-lagged, but I didn't have time to wait, so I headed straight for the office. Just outside of Boston, a city like many others hoping to repeat the magic of Silicon Valley by attracting tech companies, had been just on the start of that growth when I built my building.

I spent a lot of my time on the flight reflecting on what would happen when I got to the office. I knew morale was virtually nonexistent. Employees know when something is going on, even if they might not know exactly what that thing is. Everyone knew that, financially, the company was hemorrhaging money and that while I had been pouring in the bulk of the money I'd made in our heyday, there was a limit to what I could do. At some point or another, it would all end.

Not the healthiest of work environments to be in.

I had called Sam, my right hand, my assistant, and the only real reason the company hadn't already imploded. She basically ran the company in my absence and often ran it better than I could when I was there. I asked her to set up a meeting with the senior staff. We were a small but lean software application company, and while most of the staff fell under the development department, we also had sales, finance, IT/support, and marketing. First, however, I wanted a meeting with her.

As I walked through the front door and down the hall to my office, I received some polite hellos and some "welcome back" comments, but I could sense that they were couched in uncertainty. I had been gone far longer than my trip should have taken, and everyone knew the outcome had not been positive from the London deal that wasn't.

I could feel the tension in the air. It was electric, even if everything on the surface looked normal.

I got to my office and parked my luggage against my coat rack, not even bothering to hang up my coat but just plumping it down over my luggage. I was exhausted.

Sam walked in with a notepad and pen and took a second to look me up and down. "You don't look good."

"I know," I said, and surprised her by smiling. "Don't worry, it's jet lag. I just didn't sleep much on the plane." I closed the door behind her. "Sit down. I need to talk to you."

I knew she must be thinking this was the end. Whether she found this merciful or frightening I couldn't tell, but I didn't have time to worry about finding the right way to do this, I just had to do it.

I grabbed the chair next to her and turned it to face her. The gesture surprised her even more, as normally I always stayed behind my desk.

"I need to apologize to you," I said, looking her straight in the eye.

She leaned back in her chair a little, turning her head slightly as she said, "What for?"

I half laughed. "For a lot of things, Sam, but for now I'm just going to start with apologizing for being an idiot."

She frowned a little, unsure of what to make of me. I kept going. "Look, something happened in London. I can't go into all of it just yet, but the main thing is that it's made me realize how much I've screwed this company up. More specifically how much I've screwed up with the people who work here."

"OK," she said warily, dragging the word out.

"You're at the top of that list, Sam, and I'm really, truly, and honestly sorry."

She squirmed uncomfortably in her seat. I had never been this direct with her before. "Look, Ethan, it's fine, whatever happened, it's OK."

"No, it's not," I said, "but it's going to be. I'm going to make some changes, and I'll get to all that in a minute, but first I want to talk about you." I paused, not sure how to go about this, so I just plunged ahead somewhat blindly and hoped I wouldn't screw it up. "This is going to sound weird, and I know, I mean I *know*, that things around here have been really bad for . . . well, a long time, so bear with me for a minute, OK."

She nodded once, very slowly.

I laughed softly. "I honestly don't know why you're still here, and I wouldn't blame you at all if you've been looking or maybe already found somewhere else to work. Anyway . . ." I paused, taking a deep breath. "I want you to think about your job here. If you could do anything, and I mean anything, what would you do here?"

"Ethan, I don't . . ." she began.

"I know," I said, cutting her off. "Just think about it. I'll explain in a minute, but what kind of work do you really want to do? Where would you like to see yourself a year from now, three years, five years, *if* you were still working here?"

It took a little while to get there. I had to keep bringing her back to the question, because it was so startling for her, so out of character for me, and probably the last thing she had been thinking about. She kept asking me why I wanted to know, and I kept pushing back.

Eventually she sighed, put down her pad and pen on the edge of my desk, and said, "OK. The truth?"

I nodded.

"Yeah, things around here have been bad. Everyone is miserable, me included. And yeah, I thought about leaving, and I have looked. Well, half looked. I mean, I wasn't really trying to find another job, more just going through the motions."

She paused, probably gauging my reaction, but I just nodded encouragingly.

"The thing is, Ethan, I'm still here because of you. I know how hard you've been trying to figure a way out, and I know that even though you suck at showing it, you care about all of us."

I was touched that she knew but laughed at the "you suck" comment.

She smiled too, then continued, "I'm here because I believe in the guy who hired me. The guy whose vision we all bought into when we joined this company. The people who are still here—OK, some of the people who are still here—we believe in you. I'd be lying, though, if I didn't tell you that some of that belief is waning. We're all tired, and we're all scared."

She stopped then and took a deep breath. I could see how hard it had been for her to tell me.

I nodded, then tried to smile, though it came out a little lopsided. "Thank you. I appreciate you trusting me enough to tell me that. I don't know that my actions and behavior of late deserve it, but I am so grateful for all of you."

I leaned forward, my arms resting on top of my knees. "I'm not sure how just yet, but I'm working on some things. We need to make some pretty big changes and fast, and I'm going to need your help. I know that isn't much of anything in the way of an explanation, and I know I'm asking you to trust me, but I'm going to put everything I have into this and give it the best shot I possibly can give it."

For the next forty-five minutes, I told her about Violet and Felicity, what I knew of HABBIT21 so far, and that although I had no idea if Violet's program was going to save us or not, I was going all in on it.

She asked some questions. Really good questions. Some of which I had answers to and others that I made notes to ask Violet about because I just didn't know. Sam was hearing these things from me, the boss who was never around and had been scattered on those rare times I was in the office, so it wasn't exactly having the same impact it had had on me coming from Felicity and Violet. At the same time, there was something there. It was the way she sat a little straighter in her chair. The edge in her voice when she asked the questions.

She might not be convinced yet, more just testing the waters first, but I'd take it.

If this was going to work, I needed her help most of all.

We had about an hour before meeting my executive staff, so we spent it brainstorming the best way to present the changes. Sam was still trying to process things, so it was mostly me giving ideas and her being the sounding board and bouncing back with changes or ways to make the presentation more effective. This was how we had been in the beginning, and as the time of the meeting got closer, it hit me we that were back to being the duo we had once been.

"Hey," I said, "you never answered my question."

I didn't have to tell her which question; she knew. She had been standing by the window. Now she turned to face me. "I know. I wanted to think about it, but I know the answer now."

I waited.

"I loved working here when I started. You and I used to plan and come up with ideas, think about the future, what might come next. You gave me a lot of authority when you left, but you took that part of what we used to do with you."

She paused and I could see and feel the sadness in her voice.

"I miss that," she said. "What I would love to do is help you save this company. Not just save it, but help it thrive, take it to places we used to talk about. And . . ." She paused and took a deep breath. "I want to run this company for you one day."

Violet pulled up her message app on her phone. Ethan had sent some questions that his staff had asked over the past few days. She read through them and smiled. The questions were nothing unusual, nothing others hadn't asked before, but it meant that at least some of his staff were engaging. That was a good sign.

Her fingers flew as she answered them one by one, sending several responses one after the other. In her last message, she asked if he had time for a call to catch up later. He responded that now was a good time.

When she called, he answered right away. "Hi there, how are you?"

"I'm well. Sounds like your employees are engaging with the first three Pillars."

"Yeah," he said. "It's going to take a while, but we're off to a good start."

He told her about his meeting with his assistant Sam on the day he had flown back, and how they had put together a plan on how to best integrate the first three Pillars. The easiest thing they decided, was to talk to the executive team one-on-one, and discern which of the employees in the company needed to go.

"That wasn't an easy thing to do," Ethan said. "In fact, Sam and I spent more time trying to decide if one executive needed to stay or not."

"Really?" Violet said. "And what did you figure out?"

She heard Ethan take a deep breath. She could also hear him fidgeting with something on his desk. At least she assumed he was at his desk; it sounded like the clicking of a pen. "Well, since we haven't been practicing HICCUPs nor do we have IPF in place, we didn't feel like it would be fair to fire them out of the blue."

Violet resisted an impulse to weigh in, knowing what she knew was coming in the next Pillar, so she kept quiet. Ethan talked about how after meeting with the executives, they identified one employee who definitely needed to go and two others whom they would need to have open and honest IPS conversations with immediately.

Overall, Ethan said they were feeling pretty good about the third Pillar.

"We've got some work to do, though, on the first two."

"Go on," she said matter-of-factly.

"Well, I'm trying as best as I can to help the managers understand the merits of not having annual performance reviews, and while they seem to grasp the concept, they don't

seem too excited about implementing the IPF conversations with their subordinates."

"That's completely normal," Violet said, imagining the lines on Ethan's face scrunching up with worry. "The best way you can help them is by showing them."

"What?" Ethan replied. "You mean I should start having conversations with their subordinates for them? I wouldn't even know what to praise or correct. I mean, I'm not that involved in the details of each department."

Violet laughed. "No, Ethan. I mean show them by practicing IPF with them. If you get to know them, having regular, meaningful, open, and honest conversations with them, in time, they will see what you want them to do."

There was such a length of silence that for a moment Violet thought the call had dropped.

Finally, Ethan cleared his throat and said, "Right. Makes sense."

They talked a little while longer. It soon became apparent that there was nothing left to say, and yet Ethan kept finding reasons to continue the conversation.

Violet was listening intently to everything Ethan had been saying. Her mind processed the words, compartmentalized them, answered appropriately when needed—but it was also searching for clues. There was something she just could not put her finger on, and her mind was moving faster and faster trying to find out what it was. Something was off. Something wasn't fitting into the datasets she had collected, and she feared unless she could find the answer, it could derail the entire trajectory of her efforts in trying to help save his company.

They finally hung up. Violet sat on the bench in the small and remote park she often frequented during the day when she was back in Colorado. Her mind reviewed every detail of their conversation. She was reworking some of his nuanced answers, the pitch and tones of his voice, the moments he became *passionate or excited and those he seemed disconnected, when her phone buzzed. A text from Ethan.*

It read: **Is everything set for St. Louis?**

She responded quickly to let him know that all the arrangements had been made and that her office would send him details in the morning.

As she sat on her bench, watching a bird fly low over the small lake in front of her, it took some time before she recognized she had momentarily stopped incessantly replaying the conversation and was just sitting in the sun with a smile on her face.

Chapter 8
Wyatt

I landed at the St. Louis Lambert International Airport just before ten in the morning. I texted Violet to let her know I was on the ground. She told me which door to come out of and met me at the rideshare stop with Raphael, her Uber driver.

I gave Violet a hug, which she received as awkwardly as I was giving it. We climbed into the back of Raphael's new-looking red Nissan Murano and headed for I-70 toward the famous Gateway Arch.

Violet asked how things were going, and I filled her in on some events of the last few days as she alternated her gaze from the side window to the front, to me, to the front, and back to the side.

The twenty-minute drive ended as we pulled up in front of the Hyatt Regency St. Louis at the Arch hotel. After Violet told Raphael she would be back shortly, we got out and walked past Ruth's Chris Steakhouse awning into the lobby of the hotel.

The lobby had gleaming marble floors and bustled with people wearing conference lanyards around their necks. Suddenly a booming voice said, "Veee!"

Violet and I turned to see a hulking man with a huge smile on his face approaching with open arms. He wore a gray suit with a light blue shirt and a pink tie. Violet looked tiny as he gave her an extended bear hug. After releasing her, he continued to look down at her with his wide smile and beaming blue eyes.

Violet held onto his forearms and smiled back, then turning, she said, "Wyatt, meet Ethan. Ethan, Wyatt."

He reached out his hand, and I shook it. He had a firm grip, matching his nearly six-and-a-half-foot frame. I imagined he might be the size of a football linebacker, though it didn't look to me like Wyatt was as much an athlete as a fan of good food.

"Hello, Ethan," he said, in a thick Southern accent. "It's a pleasure to meet you."

"Likewise," I said, matching his grin. His bonhomie was contagious.

Violet said to Wyatt, "You guys get to work, and I'll meet you for lunch later and we can catch up, OK?"

Wyatt smiled back, lifted his hand with two fingers to his forehead in a mock salute, and said, "Yes, ma'am," in his Southern drawl. Just like that, Violet vanished, and I stood in the middle of the hotel with the man I'd just met.

He must have caught me looking at the conference badge hanging from the lanyard around his neck, because he took it off and said, "I've had about as much of this nonsense as I can stand. What do you say we go for a walk?"

I told him that sounded good. The weather was beautiful outside with the sun shining through bright blue skies, and I'd been cooped up in a plane all morning. I had no bags, as Violet had said this would be a one-day trip, so we walked out of the hotel and into Luther Ely Smith Park. According to the signs, we were headed toward the famous arch.

After politely asking how my flight had been, Wyatt said, "Well, we'd best get to work so's we don't get into any trouble with miss Vee." Without waiting for an answer, he went on, "As I understand things, you've already learned about the first three Pillars."

It was more of a statement than a question, so I said nothing, but I nodded in agreement. Wyatt continued, "You're gonna notice a common theme as you learn about this program that little lady put together, but before we get to that, let's talk about Pillar number four."

We parted slightly as a mother with two peacefully sleeping babies in a double-wide stroller walked between us.

"Are you familiar with the term 'funambulism'?" he asked.

I had a nagging thought that I had heard it before but couldn't recall what it meant. "No," I said, shaking my head.

"A funambulist," he said, still smiling that warm smile that seemed constantly etched onto his face, "is a tightrope walker."

I nodded.

"The fourth Pillar is what Vee calls 'Funambulist Management,'" Wyatt said. "It has a couple of components to it. The first is what I like to think of as playing human Tetris."

I looked over at him and smiled at his reference to one of my favorite old games.

"You see, Ethan, when it comes to people and business, our job as managers and leaders is simple. When you boil it all down, it comes to one thing." Wyatt raised his left index finger to illustrate his point. "Our job," he continued, "is to help people be the best version of themselves."

I thought that was an oversimplification, but I had

learned by now that keeping my mouth shut and my opinions to myself was better than the alternative where this program was concerned, so I simply nodded.

We were crossing the wide pedestrian bridge over I-44. We headed off to the side, around the viewing pavilion and onto the Gateway Arch Trail. The enormous sixty-three-story arch loomed before us as it stood watch over the Mississippi River.

Wyatt paused and looked up at the largest man-made monument in the Western Hemisphere, a testament to the vision of President Thomas Jefferson. "It never gets old," he said.

Taking in the grandeur of the "Gateway to the West," I said, "I can't imagine it does."

"Anyway," he said as we continued our walk, "for most of the last several decades, we have treated people as a commodity. We hired them to work for us, put them into a specific job, and then expected them to stay there until they retired."

He looked over as if to check that I was paying attention. I was.

"The problem, of course, is that people are changing, and our business culture is changing. One problem with this old model is that people don't stay in organizations very long anymore. The second problem," he added, "is that we never considered that one job might not be the best fit for an employee, nor the best way to help them become that best version of themselves."

I nodded again silently, using my newfound skill of "if it isn't broken, stick with it."

"Here's where the Human Tetris comes in," Wyatt said, his smile widening even further. "Since we know our employees may not stay with us for a long period of time, we need to make sure we have them working in the best possible positions for us *and* them." He jutted his arm and pointed his index finger straight up into the air for emphasis.

"We've been going at it all wrong," he said. "All this time we were trying to get the most *out* of our employees instead of helping them get the most out of themselves. Like the game of Tetris, it is about getting the tiles to fit into the correct slot of the puzzle. We need to help our employees fit into the right slots in our organizations.

"We do that," he said, barely pausing for breath, "by helping them understand their talents and strengths. Then, we work with them to find those places in our organization that best use those attributes and match their own desires and interests."

Holding up his index finger again, he said, "Notice I said places, plural, not singular."

I hadn't caught it when he said it, and I looked over at him now, curious.

"Sometimes," Wyatt said, "people don't work out in one position, and we need to move them to another."

We had passed by the side of the arch and were making our way across Leonor K. Sullivan Boulevard to the Riverwalk.

"Wait," I said, now grasping where he was going. "You're saying we need to move people around inside our organization like Tetris pieces?"

Wyatt could hear the skepticism in my voice, and he smiled again as he said, "Inside *and* outside."

I stopped in my tracks and shook my head like I was trying to get rid of a fly buzzing around me. "What?"

Wyatt placed his hand gently on my shoulder and ushered me forward as we walked beside the wide and muddy Mississippi River. "We've been so caught up in the downsizing, upsizing, accomplish-more-at-any-cost pace of doing business that we've neglected the very people who make our businesses run."

I nodded impatiently; I got that part already.

Perhaps sensing my frustration, Wyatt got to the point. "And in that process, when we *do* focus on our employees, we only focus on what they can do for us, not what we can do for them."

I looked at the large paddle-wheel riverboats docked by the quay as we passed.

"You see, Ethan," Wyatt went on, "it's not enough to just help people find the right position for their skills and passions inside our organization. The real secret is figuring out when they don't belong in our organization and helping them move on to find a better fit at another organization."

I stopped walking and turned to face him. "Look," I said, a little more sarcastically than I had intended, "I get figuring out that someone doesn't belong in my company. I see how moving them to another department can be beneficial, and maybe they'll succeed there when they were struggling at the first position they were in. I get all that." I spread my arms open, palms facing upward. "But I don't see how helping them go to another company, especially since it could be my competition, is going to help me at all. Seems to me that the only person that helps is them."

"I didn't get it either," Wyatt replied, "at first. And wait till you hear this." His Cheshire Cat–like grin was in full force as he said, "Not only do you help them move on to another organization, but you keep them employed until they find that better fit."

Wyatt stood and smiled down at me as I shook my head in bewilderment. Maybe Violet was crazy after all. I mean, I was ready to admit that the first three Pillars made more sense than I had originally given them credit for, but this one . . . this one I just wasn't sure made any sense at all.

Wyatt clapped me on the shoulder, and we turned to continue along the side of the ole Mississippi. "Here's the secret, Ethan," he said. "If someone doesn't fit at your organization, and you believe they're still an asset—maybe you've tried a couple of different positions or maybe you figured it out right away—either way, you both decide it's time they moved on. The *right* thing to do is help them. Keep them employed while they are free"—and here Wyatt really emphasized his next words—"*with your consent*, to look for another company to work for. At the same time, you're looking to hire someone else to replace them. With any luck, you'll have a little overlap so that the new employee can learn from the outgoing one."

"Yeah," I said, "I see how that helps them, but now I'm paying for two employees at the same job at the same time. Sorry, Wyatt, that just doesn't make sense."

"That's because you're still looking down at the tightrope."

I looked over at him as if he had just spoken Martian.

He laughed good-naturedly at my expression. Pointing his finger at my chest, he said, "You're still worried about that bottom line. That's the tightrope that the funambulist must walk across. Focus on the people, Ethan," he said, his tone and his expression turning very serious for a moment.

As we approached the I-64/I-55 overpass, we turned back onto the Gateway Arch Trail and began walking around the pond in the small park. Wyatt's voice remained serious as he continued, "You want to be *that* kind of company, Ethan. You want people to talk about how well you treat your employees. So well that when they leave you help them go, with your thanks and your blessing as you help them find something more suited to them."

This time he stopped walking, and I turned to face him. "Think about the kind of employees you're going to attract when word gets out that your top priority is taking care of them, their passions, their desires, their needs as human beings, not as mere cogs in the wheel of your company."

I had to admit again that he had me thinking differently about this Pillar and my own focus.

"When you can help people be the best version of themselves," Wyatt said as we continued walking, "you attract better people, more passionate people. People who want to work with you, who will enjoy their work more, and do you know what that leads to?"

Without waiting for an answer, he said, "It leads to better outcomes, better performance, and growth, and isn't that, after all, the bottom line you seem so worried about and focused on?"

We walked on in silence for a few minutes before he said, "The most dangerous thing the funambulist can do is look down at the wire. He must keep focused on the point he's trying to reach, constantly feeling where his foot is being placed, balancing the pole in his hands, but never letting his eyes veer from the destination. In that same vein, Ethan, when you focus on your people instead of the bottom line, while feeling and adjusting as you go along, then your focus is on your greatest asset, and they, after all, are what will help you reach your destination."

I was nodding along with him now. I was starting to get it.

"The second component of being a funambulist," he said, "is mostly for the managers and leaders who work for you."

I had forgotten he had mentioned that there were two parts.

"You see," Wyatt said, "when you are both a manager who has people working under you, and a boss whom you yourself work for, you must also walk the tightrope. Along with focusing on your people, you also must be a buffer between them and your supervisor. Oftentimes, the boss doesn't understand the inner workings of a department, and so if something isn't going well, or at least not the way the boss wants, they'll want to blame the department for it. The head of that department must take the brunt of the boss's displeasure."

He turned to look at me, making sure I was paying attention, which I most definitely was. "That ire coming down from above must not reach the employees directly. The department head will get the credit when things go right and must take the blame when things go wrong. The old adage of 'the buck stops here' applies not just at the top, but at every level of management.

"By walking that tightrope of managing both up and down," he continued, "you build trust in your people. They know when they screw up, and they'll know when their manager is getting in trouble. When that manager doesn't let it all 'roll downhill' but instead comes back and helps correct, adjust, and fix the problems that need to be fixed—but from a place of leadership and not authority—the result will be not only a dramatic improvement but a powerful effect on the team as well."

Again, we walked a little in silence as he let his words sink in and I tried to take in this new approach to how I thought about, and managed, the people in my company.

"Any questions on the fourth Pillar?" Wyatt said finally.

My head was swimming, and I was sure I had a lot of questions, but I couldn't find one to put into words. Wyatt saved me by saying, "Well, you think about it. We can go over things in more detail over lunch. Now, let's talk about the fifth Pillar, Transication."

I frowned. "What does Transication mean?"

"Actually, it's a made-up word."

Now I didn't feel so stupid.

"Violet made it up," he said, "because the word transparency has been so overused lately that it seems to have lost its meaning for most people."

I nodded, as I had to agree with that. Transparency had become the buzzword of the year, and people who claimed to be transparent were often anything but.

"It means," Wyatt said, interrupting my thoughts, "transparent communication, in every sense of those two words. You remember in the first Pillar, hiring people who are better at their jobs than you?" he asked.

"Yes."

"Well, this builds off that," he said. "One mistake organizations make is that even when they manage to hire the right people, that's all they do."

"What do you mean?"

Smiling his usual smile, Wyatt went on, "Often, as CEOs or presidents, or whatever it is we 'bosses' like to call ourselves, we think we have to know everything about everything, and in doing so, we think we're the only ones who can possibly have the right answers to the challenges our organizations face."

I nodded. This was one factor that made being at the top such a lonely position. Everything was up to you. Success or failure was largely my responsibility, which was one reason owning my own company, let alone being the head of it, was so stressful.

"That, of course, is the problem," Wyatt said. "Just because we see the 'big picture'—he used air quotes as he said it—"we think we're the only ones who can possibly come up with the right answer or direction or whatever. Not only is that arrogant, but it's flat out the wrong way to wrangle the steer, if you get my meaning."

I wasn't sure I understood his analogy, but I nodded anyway.

"Here's the point," he said, getting serious again. "If you hire someone who is the best at what they do, and then you make decisions that affect what they do without at least having them be part of the discussion, does that seem smart to you?"

"Well," I answered sheepishly, "when you put it that way."

"What other way is there to put it?" Wyatt said, holding his palms up. "We hire these people because they are the best people we can get to do their jobs. Jobs that we either don't know how to do or can't do as well because we're too busy doing all our CEO things. Whatever they are," he added, chuckling to himself.

"So why wouldn't we bring in the smartest people in the room and ask for their advice?" he asked, raising his right eyebrow as he looked at me. "Why don't we consult with our own experts in our own company?

"I'll tell you why," he said, before I could open my mouth to answer. "Because we're afraid. We're afraid they'll think less of us. We're afraid to let them in on the secret. We're afraid to let go of that power of knowledge we think we have.

"I'll tell you something else." He was getting more passionate as he talked. "Your employees already know most of the secrets and are smarter than you give them credit for. If you bring them in and ask for their help, they won't think less of you. They'll think more of you. Transication is about being transparent with everything, and I mean *everything*."

"Everything like . . . ?" I asked.

"Like everything!" he said, emphasizing his point. "In my company, I don't hold back. Everyone knows how we're doing financially. They know what our goals are, what our long-term strategy is. They know every action plan we have because they helped to create all of it."

He looked at me with a proud smile on his face.

I wasn't sure how I was supposed to react, so I just half-nodded and smiled back.

"I'll tell you something else," he said as we reached our starting point in front of the observation area of the arch. "Everyone in my company knows exactly what everyone else, including me, earns."

I stopped in my tracks at that one. "Seriously?"

"Absolutely," he said with a straight face this time. "Look, you know how business always talked a good game about fair pay, equal pay for women?" he asked, again raising his eyebrow. "Ha. That's a laugh."

"Doesn't having all your salaries out in the open like that cause problems though?"

"Like what?" he answered, but then went on, "Like having someone publish the information out on the internet?"

I nodded with a smirk. "Yeah, like that."

"Been there, done that," he said to my surprise. "Happened soon after we started our Transication policy, and you know what? It backfired. The other employees found out who did it and gave the guy a ton of grief over it. Turns out they didn't mind their coworkers knowing how much they made, but they didn't want their family to know."

Wyatt laughed out loud.

"Look," he said, "if we're going to be transparent, then we're going all in. If Joe works next to Sally and they have the same background, tenure, experience, whatever, and Joe sees Sally is making more than him, what does that mean?"

I shrugged, not sure where he was going.

"In the old way of doing business, Joe would get angry, go into his supervisor's office to complain, maybe file a grievance, who knows, but it would cause problems because the discrepancy would seem unfair. But"—Wyatt held up a finger—"because we are relentless about practicing HICCUPs and the manager is constantly having conversations with Joe about how he's doing, Joe knows exactly why he's not making as much as Sally. It's because Sally is kicking his butt." Wyatt grinned.

"We also believe in SPOOFing," he said. "The first three letters stand for Succeed Publicly and Often. We're very public about when someone's doing something good so that everyone sees it. It's not only great to give credit where credit is due, but it helps model what we want others to do as well."

Wyatt suggested we walk a few blocks to Charlie Gitto's, one of his favorite Italian restaurants, where we would meet Violet for lunch.

"The last two letters of SPOOFing," he said as we set off from the park, "have to do with being really Open about Failure."

I laughed out loud. "Really?"

He smiled back. "Yes. It's all part of Transication. We want our people to be OK with trying new things, and we let them know that it's OK if they fail."

He held up his hand just as I was about to speak. "All within reason, of course." He chuckled. "We don't want people to get stuck in failure, but we want them to know that we encourage thinking outside the box. We encourage them to attempt, to explore, and if it doesn't work, well, it's like that old boy Edison once said, just another way he learned about how not to make the lightbulb." Then Wyatt smiled his broad smile again. "But eventually, he figured it out."

Still smiling, he added, "When we're open about failure, we also educate everyone on something that doesn't work. It helps keep people from repeating it in the future."

———— • ⧒⧓ • ————

Violet arrived at Charlie Gitto's about five minutes after Wyatt and Ethan were seated, and they both got up as she approached the table. She took in, as always, the multitude of people, the sights and the sounds throughout the restaurant as she made her way over. She also took in the looks from other guests—some because of her dress, some because she was female and men can't help themselves, and some out of pure curiosity.

She received another bear hug from Wyatt and when she turned to Ethan, he hugged her as well, though somewhat awkwardly, mirroring her own reaction. Still, she smiled at him and then sat down, quickly beginning her scan of the room to take in all the data required to satisfy her mind's constant need for information.

Wyatt was his usual jovial self. Violet always loved his good-humored approach to life, and as they finished ordering their lunch from the server, she watched as the two men continued their conversation.

Ethan was digging deeper into the subject of the Funambulist Management Pillar.

"It still doesn't make sense though," he was saying. "I mean, if an employee is leaving my organization, why is it my responsibility to help them?"

As Violet continued to look around at the stereotypical Italian decor of the restaurant, she caught Wyatt shooting her a quick glance before he said, "There's a Hawaiian word, kuleana, have you ever heard of it?"

Ethan shook his head.

"It doesn't have a literal translation, but the essence of the word is this: You have the right to what you want in life, and with that right comes great responsibility.

"I think it's a great word for business as well. You see, Ethan, you have the right to expect your employees to give their all, to help you in your business, to provide great customer service, et cetera, et cetera, et cetera," Wyatt said. *"And with that right comes the responsibility of taking care of your employees."*

Ethan leaned forward, his forearms resting on the table, and Violet noted his earnest expression as he almost cut Wyatt off by saying, *"Yes, and I agree with that part of it. But once the determination is made that an employee is leaving, or should leave, or what have you, doesn't my responsibility end at that point? I mean, they're no longer going to be working for me. Shouldn't they just leave, and we part ways?"*

Wyatt glanced at Violet, which caused Ethan to turn and look at her as well. As soon as he did, his eyes darted down. Then he slowly looked up again, blinking and glancing away a few times.

Violet took all of this in, then said, *"That's the traditional way of managing. Looking down at the bottom line, focusing on the proverbial 'what's best for the company.'"*

Again, Ethan chimed in almost before she had finished. *"Look, I'm not trying to be a jerk here. I get that this is about what's best for the employee. I just don't see why I, as the company, should be on the hook for it."*

Violet stopped her wandering gaze for a moment and looked him directly in the eye. *"What you're struggling with is that you can't see why you should do the right thing by the employee?"*

She could see him squirming. A fleeting thought passed through her mind amid the multiple data points it was processing: *Is he squirming because of the question, because of my direct look, or both?*

Ethan took a deep breath and looked from Violet to Wyatt and back. *"I'm not saying this right. OK, say I 'do the right thing,' so what? I mean, it costs me more money, the employee gets a free ride while they look for another job, and meanwhile, they'll probably have that lame duck attitude of every employee who is about to leave or retire or whatever. Their productivity will go down, they'll get 'short-termer-itis,' and all I get is the knowledge that I get to pat myself on the back for 'doing the right thing.'" Ethan held up air quotes when he said the last four words.*

"Yes," Violet answered matter-of-factly.

Ethan just stared at her dumbfoundedly. He looked at Wyatt, who simply smiled broadly back at him.

Violet could see the shocked expression on Ethan's face. She could almost hear the thoughts swirling in his brain. The same thoughts Felicity and Wyatt and everyone else had when they reached this conclusion.

She chanced a quick glance left and right, registering more people who were coming and going before turning her full attention back to Ethan. "And if that was all there was, would it be enough?" she asked.

She watched as the inevitable process played out before her eyes. Ethan slowly shook his head back and forth. Finally, taking another deep breath, he looked at both of them and with an almost defeated tone and said, "I guess. I mean, I'm trying to keep an open mind here, and if you're both telling me that doing the right thing is what I need to do, then I guess I'll just . . ."

Violet was watching the pupils of his golden-brown eyes. Her focus had become laser-like, and while she knew it could be disturbing to have someone looking at you so intently, she also knew his mind was too preoccupied with the conversation to fully take in the intensity of her gaze. And so, when it happened, she knew it before his brain even registered it.

She watched as his pupils widened ever so slightly, even though the light in the room had not changed. It took a millisecond for his eyes to react as his brain processed the thought, then his focus narrowed, and he was able to look directly back at her. "Wait . . . you said, 'IF that was all there was.'"

Violet allowed herself a small smile and glanced at Wyatt, who chuckled and nodded as he took a sip of his water.

Ethan looked at them both, and then, trying to match the look Violet was giving him, waited for her to reply.

"The first time this happens," she said, her voice still intense but less stern than before, "you're right. The only benefit you'll have, at least tangibly, is to be able to say to yourself that you did the right thing."

She could almost feel his anticipation as he waited for her to continue, now that he knew there was more than that to this Pillar. "Except you won't just be saying it to yourself. You'll also be saying it to the entire organization.

"Employees notice everything," she continued. "When you help that first employee leave, with honor, and support, and grace . . . they will pay attention.

"It might not be the first one, or the second one, or even the third one; but eventually, it will resonate. Every employee will realize that unless they do something illegal or detrimental to the organization, the organization will take care of them, even if it means they have to leave.

"And when that happens, Ethan, the entire culture changes." She didn't give him a chance to say anything, adding, "The next time an employee must leave after that culture shift and you help them do so, that employee won't have a loss in productivity. They won't get short-term-itis. They will be truly and authentically grateful."

Wyatt chimed in. "When my employees finally got it, the next guy who left didn't just check out. He worked his butt off. We practically had to kick him out of the office at the end of his last day. He kept saying he had just a couple more things he wanted to finish before he left."

Violet watched as Ethan began to recognize the value of the bigger picture. She gave him a moment, then when she saw him blink and knew he was listening intently again, she said, "That's when word will start to spread. That's when the people who apply to work for you, and get hired, will be the ones who have heard about this employee-focused culture and want to work there. And when they start," she said, preempting Ethan, who had taken a breath to say something, "your current employees will model what it looks like to be in that kind of atmosphere. It won't be something anyone has to 'try' to do, it will be just how it is, and that's when the magic happens."

She watched as Ethan sat back in his seat. It was well-timed, as just then the server brought their food, placing the various pastas, salads, and bread around the table.

Taking a sip of his iced tea, Ethan slowly set the glass back down as he formulated what he wanted to say. Violet turned to watch the server stop by the table of a family with children. She took in the sight of each child, what they were eating, how they were sitting, how the mother was helping one child and the father was trying to control another while telling the server that everything was fine. Violet absorbed every detail while still keeping the focus of her hearing on her own table.

Ethan started to speak, and her gaze returned and focused on him. She watched him stumble as their eyes met. He swallowed, then said, "It just . . . I don't know . . . It sounds too good to be true."

Both Violet and Ethan turned to Wyatt as he chuckled. "Man, do I remember thinking that. Look, it doesn't mean you'll have perfect employees. People are still people, and there are good ones and bad ones, good days and bad days.

"What it does mean, though, is that in the long run you'll have better employees, and they will actually care about the company. About what happens to it. And ultimately, I'm telling you, the entire business culture will just get better. It creates a better work environment."

Not for the first time, Violet smiled inwardly at the age-old notion that once you learned something well, the best thing to do was teach another person what you knew. She loved how the Wyatts of the world she had worked with were ambassadors of her HABBIT21 program who could now effortlessly communicate its merit to others. This was how movements began. This was what she had hoped for all along, to transform business, and she was watching it happen in real time right before her eyes.

Chapter 9
Transication

I took a bite of my lasagna. I have a rule that whenever I am in an Italian restaurant for the first time, I try their lasagna as a measuring stick for how good their food is. This one was good. Nothing special in terms of how it was prepared—it was pretty typical in that regard—and yet they had gotten everything right.

I had been engaging with Wyatt, going deeper and deeper into the fourth Pillar, and I realized just as he was finishing his last point, Violet had gone quiet. Nothing had changed in her demeanor. She was still canvassing the room by turning her head, and even when her head did not move, her eyes were constantly roving. I watched as she occasionally glanced past Wyatt and me, only to continue searching for whatever it was she was trying to find.

Just as suddenly as her eyes had glanced over me and moved on, they swung back, and I felt the full force of her stare. I glanced down at my food, nervous and embarrassed that she had caught me looking at her. After a few seconds, I looked up, but over toward Wyatt, trying with all my might to use my peripheral vision to see if she was still looking at me.

To my horror, not only was she still looking, but she had also put her hands down and was no longer eating. She was giving me the full force of her stare.

Panicking, I glanced at her then back at Wyatt, and as if I was purposefully speaking to both of them, I said, "Can we talk about the fifth Pillar, because I have to tell you, this whole transparency thing makes me want to cringe."

Wyatt, who thankfully was oblivious to the stare Violet was giving me, saved me and said, "Is it about the transparency of salaries?"

"Yes!" I said a little too quickly. Then, trying to come up with something intelligent, I added, "I guess I'm just afraid that my employees won't appreciate having their lives outed, if you know what I mean, at least about their salaries."

Wyatt smiled, put down his fork, and said, "Absolutely. You have to understand that you're not just going to go back to your office and send out an email or post everything on an intranet. You prepare and plan for this." Then, turning to Violet, he added, "Right, Vee?"

Now I had to look at her, and when I did, I met her eyes as they looked straight into mine. I couldn't read her expression. She didn't look upset or even concerned, but there was something behind her look I couldn't place.

There was silence for what seemed like a long time. Long enough that Wyatt cleared his throat as though to speak. Suddenly Violet began looking around the room and said, "In your case, Ethan, I think you're going to have to plan this far in advance. Probably something like six months."

She turned her head back to me and said, "You're going to need to prepare your staff for what's coming, explain to them why, what, and when. Give them time to adjust to what is going to happen, let some of them get their questions out, and then decide on a date and pull the Band-Aid off."

I nodded, mostly because I felt like I was supposed to. "Can you just help me understand why this is so important? I guess I'm not sure I get it."

Violet turned to Wyatt and said, "Why is it important, Wyatt?"

Without missing a beat, he said, "Businesses have for too long taken advantage of employees. They've had this almost unwritten relationship with their employees, which said, 'I'll pay you just enough so that you don't quit.'"

I smiled at that one, mostly because it sounded about right. Wyatt was only halfway done though. "And the employee, well, they're thinking, 'And I'll work just hard enough so you don't fire me.'"

I nodded my head sadly.

"Don't get me wrong," he continued. "Not everyone is like that, but business has not been honest with its workforce for a long time. The reason was because leadership feared that if employees knew how much money the corporation was making, the employees would demand more or leave disgusted by what they felt was a considerable inequity."

"And they would both have been right," Violet chimed in. She looked at Wyatt and nodded, encouraging him to continue.

"So, they kept the big picture to themselves," Wyatt said. "With the stock market and shareholders demanding ever and ever more profit, they simply felt they couldn't afford to take the chance.

"What they didn't consider, however, is that at some point, employees would stop being loyal. It didn't matter that they, the business, had never truly been loyal to the employees, or that as time went on, any reason to keep them loyal, like bonuses, or retirement plans, or pensions or what have you, went by the wayside.

"To the business, it was always about making more and more money, being more and more profitable, and as culture and workforces have continued to develop, they have tightened their belts even more, cutting costs at alarming rates."

Violet took over. "What they missed is that getting employees engaged in the big picture helps their bottom line. It's part of what Pillar four does. Most people think employees leave because they don't get paid enough. After all," she said, "most people move to another company with a higher salary than the one they left, so surely that must be it."

Wanting to sound like I wasn't a complete idiot, I said, "Yeah, I talked to Felicity about that. It's not really the main reason, right? Money is just one reason, but feeling like they matter and that their supervisor appreciates them is the big one."

"Yes," Violet said, "but let's not overlook money. Everyone who works, no matter what their job, would like to earn more."

She said it straightforwardly, though she raised her eyebrows as if questioning us or asking us to question the logic. Wyatt was just smiling, so I looked back at her and nodded slightly.

"So why not just eliminate that piece of the puzzle? When people know what's going on with the big picture, and they are paid fair and valid compensation for what they do, they will understand that the purpose of the business is to turn a profit, and that there are stakeholders to answer to in the case of a public company.

"They will also," she added, "no longer worry about favoritism, nepotism, or other company cultures that can pervade and invade an organization and send it spiraling into chaos."

"OK," I said, still skeptical, "but surely you're not suggesting that everyone is paid the same wage for the same job. This isn't socialism we're talking about here, right?"

Violet shared a look with Wyatt. He nodded at her and then, turning to me, said, "That's almost the same question I had way back when. No, that's not what this is. Of course, there will be people who do the same job but who are paid according to their performance, their skill, their levels of responsibility, et cetera . . .

"And that's where the second and fourth Pillars come in and why they are so important. What's so perfect about this, what Vee has done, is that each Pillar builds on and relies upon the others. You see, when we communicate transparently, while building authentic relationships and maintaining constant communication with our employees, having honest and open conversations with them—no one is surprised about where they fall in the hierarchy or by how much they make.

"Here's the best part." Wyatt had a glint in his eyes as he leaned forward for what he said next. "When one of my employees gets a raise, their peers are genuinely happy for them." He leaned back in his chair, opened his arms wide, and said, "When was the last time you could say that about someone else getting a promotion or a raise? Literally, the people in my company will applaud someone when they move up because they know that person deserved it and has been doing what they needed to do. There's no mystery about it. It's brilliant!"

When lunch ended, Wyatt announced he had better at least show his face at the conference this afternoon so he could pretend he had been attending. He gave Violet a hug and said, "Next time, we need to have you over for dinner or I'll be sleeping on the couch."

Violet smiled up at him. "OK, give Barbara my love, please."

"I sure will," he said. Then, turning to Ethan, he reached out and shook his hand. "Good luck, son. I know this all seems like a lot, but trust me, it's worth the effort. Put in the work and you'll be just fine." Pointing his thumb back at Violet, he added, "Trust her; she knows what she's doing."

Violet suppressed a smile as she looked up and down the street, feeling the blood and heat rising to her cheeks as she blushed from Wyatt's compliments.

After saying their goodbyes, Violet and Ethan climbed into their rideshare and headed back to the airport. Ethan seemed content to look out the window, contemplating, no doubt, much of what he had just learned.

Violet, for her part, was straining to understand this man she was trying to help. As usual, her senses were taking in everything that was happening, all the sights and sounds along their journey. Her mind, however, was processing every interaction, every conversation, every look, every moment that she had spent around him, trying to find the missing link she knew was there but couldn't grasp.

She tried sorting through things logically, taking one component at a time. His history, then his business, his mannerisms, his speech patterns, his dress. She went deeper, analyzing his cognitive abilities and his skills (as much as she had determined them from researching the "app wizard").

Round and round, her mind searched, trying to find the missing piece. There was something, something she couldn't recognize about him that her mind refused to let go. She knew from the countless hours she had spent scouring the internet that he was mostly a private man. Not prone to glitz and glamor, he didn't go out with high society or attend the "see and be seen" red carpet events that so many people of his status craved.

If he had vices, he kept them to himself.

His only visible flaw was the recent fall from grace in his business, and Violet knew he wasn't alone in this area. So many organizations were struggling to keep up with the change in working culture that was spreading all over the world.

As they arrived at the airport, she asked the driver to wait for her and got out with Ethan.

"Let's talk later," she said, and her eyes narrowed slightly as she looked straight at him. "Give some thought to what you learned today and how you might want to implement things, then we can put a plan together."

Ethan seemed relieved as his face relaxed. He took a deep breath and then glanced at the door into the airport and back at her. "OK, sounds good," he said, though his voice seemed a little strained.

There was a pause, and then he opened his arms and leaned toward her. They hugged awkwardly again, and then he turned to go inside. As he passed through the doors, Violet watched him look up at the signs to determine which way he needed to go, and just as he turned to his left, he glanced back over his shoulder. Their eyes met, and he smiled before moving out of her sight.

Violet turned to face her car and suddenly froze.

There it was. Her mind, never at ease, had just found what it had been searching for. Everything suddenly made sense, like when the multifaceted sides of the Petaminx, one of the more challenging versions of the Rubik's Cube, suddenly all fall into place.

With a speed that would have seemed blindingly fast to other people, Violet's mind processed this new discovery against every piece of data she had on Ethan. Cross-referencing, validating, checking for unknown variables and then re-cataloging and sorting everything she had been thinking about.

Her driver was staring at her through his window, another data point thrown into the never-ending input stream and stored temporarily aside. Violet stood still as the busy world of passenger drop-offs, buses, taxis, airport traffic wardens, and humanity at large continued to move in a swirl around her.

Finally, her driver rolled down his window. "Miss, are you OK?"

Violet fixed her stare on him for a few moments before shaking her head slightly and getting back in. The missing piece wasn't so much disconcerting as it was surprising. It simply had never occurred to her.

He likes me, *she thought.*

Chapter 10
Weak Spots

I was the first one in the office the next morning. I'd spent much of the return flight and the evening pondering my next steps. I went through all the employees in my head. I knew the direct reports better than the rest, but it was still clear to me where our weak spots were.

There were two people I could think of who likely needed to go. One was a direct report, and the other was someone lower down the management chain who had been a problem from day one. We weren't a good fit for either of them.

I'd called Violet late last night to ask for some advice, and together we put together a plan of sorts for how to deal with this. So, here I was, coffee in hand, staring out my window with the sun having just risen outside.

As the staff came in, people went about their usual routines. I mostly stayed in my office until Sam arrived, and I asked her to join me there. I explained everything I had learned with Pillars four and five. She listened, nodding now and again, trying to absorb everything.

"I know it's a lot," I said. She nodded and smiled. "And I know we have to talk about the Transication piece, but first we need to act on a couple of employees."

I told her the two people I was thinking of "helping" to leave. She immediately agreed and then brought up a third name. We discussed the third employee for quite a while, going back and forth on whether she should go. Ultimately, we decided to sit her down and talk to her to see if she wanted to stay or perhaps move into another department, or if she was not happy and should leave. We agreed that the first two needed to go.

I called Joe Timble, the head of our sales department, into my office. I had asked Sam to stay. Not simply because it was good to have someone in the room as a witness in case something went wrong, but as Violet and I had discussed the night before, Sam was the one I trusted most and was grooming to take over one day. More than anyone else, I needed her to buy into this new way of running the business.

Joe entered and, seeing Sam, he raised his eyebrows as he sat down in one of the chairs around my circular table. "What's up?" he asked good-naturedly.

I took a deep breath. "Joe, I've known you for what, five years now?"

He nodded. "Yeah, that sounds about right."

I jumped right in. "In those five years, when was the last time you looked forward to coming to work?"

Joe furrowed his brow. He looked at Sam (who kept a great poker face) and then back at me. "What do you mean?" he said cautiously.

Violet had told me to rip the Band-Aid off and not try to soften the blow. That was hard, but I knew she was right. "I think we both know you haven't been happy here for a long time, Joe. I think it's time we found somewhere that will suit you better."

He leaned forward, gripping the sides of his chair. "Are you firing me?"

I could see he was ready for a fight. I looked at him and said, "No, not exactly."

That made him sit up a little straighter. "What does that mean?" He was still cautious and certainly not happy about the way the conversation was going.

"It's simple," I said. "I think you would be much happier working somewhere else, and I think you know I'm right. But," I said, holding up my hand as he began to say something, "I'm not firing you."

He looked back at Sam again and smiled. Then, looking at me like I had lost my mind, he said, "So, let me get this straight, you want me to go work somewhere else, but you're not firing me?"

I smiled back at him. "Yep, that's about it." I paused and then added, "I'm not firing you because you don't have to leave until you find a new job, and I'll help you find it. I'll continue to pay you, you'll continue to do your job, but you will have free rein to look for another job, take job interviews—I'll even write you a letter of recommendation."

That knocked him back in his seat. He stared at me for a few moments, then looked over at Sam and said, "Is he serious?"

She just smiled and nodded.

Turning back to me, Joe asked, "Why would you do that? Aren't you afraid I'll take all the client files with me when I go?"

"The reason I'm doing this is because you've spent five years of your life helping me build, and then hold onto, this company. I owe you something for that, Joe. Just because you don't want to work here anymore, and it doesn't seem to be a good fit for you or for us, doesn't make those five years go away.

"I want you to be happy, Joe, and I want the person who's running my sales department to be happy too, so why not do both?" I held my hands, palms up, as I asked the question. "I'm also hoping you'll help me, for as long as you're here, to find your replacement."

He was still trying to process it all, and I could almost see his thoughts progressing when he asked, "Wait, what if you find my replacement before I find a new job?"

"Then you'll train the new person and I'll pay you both until you do."

"Are you out of your mind?" he said incredulously. I could see that the salesman in him just couldn't reconcile anyone paying two people for one job.

"Look," I said, "I honestly think it will be the other way around. You're a talented guy with an impressive track record. Our sales numbers this past year and a half haven't been your fault, they were mine. Like I said, I will write you a great letter, which you deserve, and my guess is you'll be gone before we can hire anyone to replace you."

"What about promoting someone internally?"

"If we decide to go that route, great," I said. "But if that happens, we have even more control over the timing."

I could see he was struggling with it all, so we went over it all again. Sam chimed in every now and again to help clarify points so he could better understand. She really had a good handle on how the people in the office communicated, far better than mine.

Once we got past the initial shock and assured him we were serious about how this was going to work, we threw the second curveball at him by having him fill out a form I had made early that morning. It was based on the conversation Violet and I had on the phone and basically centered on a series of questions to help him better define what he wanted to do and the type of company he wanted to work for.

He quickly came up with a few specific companies, though after writing them down he said, "They'd be great to work for, but they all have sales directors, so they won't be looking."

"You never know," I said. "Let's put out some feelers. I'll contact some people; you work your network, and we'll see what shakes out."

After filling in a few more answers on the form, Joe looked up. "How does this work with the rest of the employees and my staff?"

"We'll tell them." Seeing the alarm quickly rise in his eyes, I added, "When we're ready. For now, let's see what our feelers come back with. The three of us will sit down and talk about how and when. For now, let's just take it one day at a time."

I could see Sam's head tilt to the side a little when I said "the three of us." I just looked at her and winked, which I think surprised her more than anything.

While Joe headed back to his office scratching his head, we called in the head of our quality assurance department, Serina Gutierrez. She sat down, clearly a little unnerved about the call to my office, but I quickly began explaining the concept to her because the other two people I wanted to talk to both came from her department.

I quickly pointed out that these two people were not a reflection of her, as she had inherited both when she took the job.

Serina is wicked smart and picked up on the how and why quickly. She noted that the approach seemed too generous for the one employee and that she had been wanting to talk to me about him for some time but just couldn't get on my schedule.

The three of us talked at length about the third employee, going back and forth. Sam brought up some of the same points she had raised with me. Serina agreed that the best course was to just ask the employee and see what she thought.

So, one by one, we called the two employees in.

Chris Olson seemed almost relieved when I told him we thought he might be happier working somewhere else. I hadn't even gotten to the part where we would help him before he looked at Serina and said, "Whew. I've been looking for a job for the last two weeks, and I wasn't sure how to tell you."

I told him how we were going to help him, and Serina jumped in, filling in some of the message like we had been doing this for years, like it was standard practice. Sam caught my eye and raised her eyebrows as if to say, "Wow, look at her go."

He was speechless after we laid out how we would help him look for a job and continue to pay him for his work until he found one. If anything, he walked out of my office a little taller than he had come in.

Before we called the next person in, Serina looked at me and said, "You know, this won't take long to get out. He's gonna tell people."

I looked at Sam. She said, "There's no way to stop it, so we'll just have to get ahead of it. We'll call an all-employees meeting this afternoon and tell them about how we're doing business. No big deal, just a new policy. We'll take questions; they'll be the same ones he just asked, and then we'll see what happens. People will either embrace it or they won't, but it's how Ethan wants to run the company, so that's what we're going to do." She paused, as if unsure whether she wanted to say something else. In the end she added, "I, for one, think it's an innovative and brilliant way to treat people."

Serina smiled, then looked at me and said, "So do I."

***

With the last employee, a woman named Linda Calnor, we got straight to the point without mincing words. All three of us tag-teamed off one another to give her all the information we wanted her to know: how we weren't sure if she enjoyed the work she was doing, how we wondered if there was another department she might want to work in, or maybe another company. Serina quickly chimed in to explain how we would help her if she wanted to leave, and Sam equally quickly filled in the rest.

I sat and watched as these two women, who hadn't even had a day to absorb the notion of this new policy, embraced it so quickly and were now enacting it with very little input from me. It was astounding.

As they finished piecing together the puzzle for Linda, there was a pause, and then Linda broke down crying. Sam, Serina, and I all looked at each other in mild panic.

Linda immediately apologized, and in between sniffing and wiping her eyes with tissues, she explained she loved her job, and she was sorry for not being very focused lately. It turned out that her mother had been dealing with dementia and had moved into their home. She and her husband had been trying to juggle not only their three children and all that goes with that but also her mother's illness and the anxiety of what might happen.

We all sat stunned for a moment. None of us had any idea.

In a flash, I realized just how vital it was to do a better job of getting to know the people who work for us. If we had been practicing Transication, none of this would have been a surprise.

Almost as if on an invisible cue, Sam and Serina simultaneously reached over and assured Linda that we were going to help, that we would do everything we could to help her and her family. At one point, all three women looked up at me as if daring me to contradict what they were saying.

I agreed wholeheartedly and told her we were going to give her some paid time off to be with her mother, and that her job would be here when she got back.

She started protesting, saying she had too much to do and couldn't afford to be gone because of all the projects she had on her desk, plus they helped keep her mind off things. Serina looked at me, unsure of what to say, and I could see from her expression that what Linda was saying worried Serina as well.

I glanced at Sam, who was chewing her lower lip in thought, and half shrugged when she caught my eye.

"OK," I said, "look, we're a technology company. There has to be a way for us to figure this out. Maybe you'll work from home, or part there, part here, I don't know. I trust Serina and I'm sure she will work with you to figure out how to make this work. We want to support you, so you're going to drive this boat. You tell us how we can help you best, and it will be our job to make sure we figure out how to do that. Just know that we're here for you."

That started her crying again, but this time out of gratitude and relief.

I looked at my watch. It wasn't even eleven o'clock in the morning, and it already felt like a full day.

Violet had talked to Ethan three times in the past week. They had discussed the conversations with his employees, the hard decisions, the low-hanging fruit he had to deal with, and then they had strategized.

Each call had lasted longer than the one before it, with neither Violet nor Ethan wanting to end it. Violet consciously understood what was happening but couldn't quite find a logical basis for it.

Finally, she had called her surrogate father, Jeff. He had been her father's best friend and had taken her in after the accident that killed her parents. She had been almost three years old, and Jeff was the only father figure she had ever really known.

He was also the one who understood her best.

She had described the events of recent weeks, the restaurant, and now the calls. She asked Jeff what he thought.

He laughed.

"What?" she said, somewhat annoyed.

"I'm sorry, sweetheart," he said in his kind and always reassuring voice. "I forget sometimes that these things are hard for you; forgive me." And then he explained at length, finally summarizing for her data-starved brain the obvious point of it all. "If I had to guess, I'd say you might like him as much, if not more, than he seems to like you."

And there it was. That little data point that had always been floating around the edge of her consciousness. The thing she "knew" but didn't "know" until Jeff said it out loud. It was the strength of her affection that she hadn't picked up on. Like an intricate jigsaw puzzle where all the pieces had been floating in a giant ball in front of her mind's eye, and suddenly, slowly, precisely, they fell, one after the other, in perfect order and formed the picture on the table before her.

Her focus returned to the latest call with Ethan. As usual, it had been a video call, during which they were both often distracted by other things on their computer screens. This time, Violet was out walking in the park, her noise-canceling earbuds in and the sun on her face, holding her phone in front of her as she walked, not always keeping her face in frame because of all the distractions.

Ethan didn't seem to mind.

"So," he said, "what do you think?"

"I think it's right," she said, referring to his comment that he was going to gather his staff and get transparent about salaries.

"Do you think it will freak them out?" he asked nervously.

Violet lifted the phone and looked directly at it. "You're not going to 'out' their salaries today. You're giving them advanced notice that the day is coming." Then she stopped walking and gave the camera her full attention. "Giving them the transparency of your salary, especially the history of it, how the company got to where it is, and how you're dropping your salary to virtually nothing to keep paying them while you rebuild? No, I don't think that's going to freak them out," she said bluntly, and went back to walking, dropping the phone again. Her arm resumed swaying, and her head moved in and out of frame.

She could hear Ethan's voice in her ears. "Well, when you put it like that."

She knew he couldn't quite see her face completely, as her arm was swinging as she walked, but she knew he'd glimpsed the smile on her face.

"OK," she said with a heavy sigh, "I really have to go. Call me tonight and let me know how it went."

"I will," he said, and she could hear the twinge of sadness in his voice.

"And don't forget, next week we're headed for the last two trips."

"Bags are already packed," he said in a serious tone, and she wondered if he meant it. She hadn't even started packing. After all, they were still four and a half days away. She had plenty of time. Again, she could feel herself smile.

Chapter 11
Flight to Singapore

I met Violet at San Francisco International Airport for our flight to Singapore. Although it was a direct flight, it would take almost seventeen and a half hours to get there. Given my financial situation, I had originally planned on flying business class. I had winced at the cost, though. While certainly not as luxurious as first class, I simply couldn't stomach the thought of flying coach for that long.

Violet had insisted on making the travel arrangements through her office and surprised me by gifting me enough mileage points to bump me up to first class. As we boarded the plane, I had to admit feeling a huge wave of relief, and more than a little guilt when I thought of those who would make the trip in the seats behind us.

It was a late flight, leaving at almost 11 p.m., and we'd be arriving in Singapore just before 6 a.m., though two days in the future. We settled into our seats, which eventually turned into beds when it was time to get some rest. I'm not sure how well I slept. Despite the upgrade from a reclining seat, between the turbulence, the constant hum of the engines, and the vibrations of the plane, it was not the most fitful rest I could remember.

I awoke after about six hours and lowered the divider between our private mini-cabin seats to find Violet already sipping orange juice and working on a laptop. The attendant came by to ask what I would like for breakfast, and after eating and getting myself freshened up, I settled in to do some work as well.

Violet and I talked on and off for much of the day as our plane circumnavigated half the globe. We spoke easily and comfortably, and eventually I asked her about her past.

She paused, looking off into the distance. I waited.

"My parents died when I was almost three years old," she began, "and I was raised by the only father I ever knew. He was my dad's best friend. His name is Jeffery Holbourn. My grandparents on both sides were already dead, so Jeffery raised me as his own.

"It wasn't long before he noticed I wasn't quite the same as other kids. That's when my testing started." Violet looked at me with her eyebrows raised. "I have been in more hospitals, doctors' offices, specialists, and laboratories in the first fifteen years of my life than most people will ever go through in their lifetimes.

"I knew I didn't act like kids my age and I was constantly getting in trouble because I just didn't fit in. When I was diagnosed as being on the autistic spectrum, I could see Jeffery nodding when the doctor said the words as though it made sense." Violet paused, gauging my reaction.

I was fascinated and felt a little like I was intruding on something personal. Violet continued, "What the doctor said next, though, changed everything. He told us that while I tested on the spectrum, it was the way I tested that had him concerned. Apparently, I tested in ways—plural—that they had never seen.

"I spent the next few years seeing one specialist after another. Not just in Colorado where I'm from, but all over the country and the world. Jeffery and I went through countless inpatient and outpatient programs, learned all the coping mechanisms, but what worked on one part of my brain completely frustrated another.

"It helped, don't get me wrong," she said pointedly, "but life wasn't easy." Violet paused again, and this time a warm smile crossed her face before she continued, "I was so lucky to have Jeffery. I'm not sure how many single men would take on a kid like me, much less stick with me."

I realized that although she referred to this man as the "only father I ever knew," she only ever called him Jefferey, not Dad.

"Anyway, Jefferey had come from a background in big pharma, so he reached out, thinking maybe there might be answers there."

Maybe she saw the doubt on my face because she nodded. "Yeah, I can tell you I wasn't crazy about trying new drugs. The ones they had me on already had more side effects than the one thing they were supposed to fix. For every 'symptom'"—she used air quotes around the word—"the drug was supposed to fix, it gave me three or four other side effects I had to deal with.

"I couldn't blame Jeffery though; life was really hard back then. I was a preteen, and with all the hormones in my body making themselves heard, the poor man was at his wits' end."

I smiled, more at the thought of Violet being a preteen than at the thought of the angst that must have come to her and her father's life.

"Luckily, one of his former colleagues pointed us to another who pointed us to another who ended up introducing us to a team of scientists in Zurich. They were neuroscientists who were working on some pretty cool stuff that isn't related to people on the spectrum, but when they heard about what was happening with me, they became really interested.

"Turns out that some of their work at the cellular and molecular level within the brain had given them some ideas, and they began working on a way to help me control what was happening to me."

It was my turn to raise my eyebrows. "That's amazing," I said. "That must have cost a fortune though."

Violet smiled. "As luck would have it, I was able to help with that. I was just turning twelve, and Jeffery was reading the stock market results in the paper, and I asked him what it all meant."

She looked at me with a mischievous grin and then continued, "When he started talking about how stocks work, my brain kind of clicked on."

I looked at her with a frown. She smiled again, then added, "Over the next four or five years I began playing the stock market. Well, we did," she corrected. "Jeffery and me. The thing is, that numbers are logical sequences, and my brain really likes logic and sequences. There's something about patterns, really any pattern, but with numbers I see them much quicker than anything else.

"So, I started watching the numbers, doing my own research on companies, and I kept a spreadsheet of what I thought would go up and down. When I showed Jeffery," she said, laughing out loud at the memory, "he actually spewed the coffee he was drinking all over the table."

"How accurate were you?" I asked.

"Pretty accurate," she answered sheepishly. I decided not to press. "Anyway, it helped cover the costs and then some."

"That's amazing," I said, impressed.

"The thing is that people don't understand the variations of being on the spectrum. They typically associate the spectrum with extremes they've seen in movies like *Rain Man* or whatever," she said. "I once saw a quote on social media that I really liked. It said, 'It isn't a processing error. It's a whole different operating system.' And I think that might be the best explanation I've ever seen."

I thought about that for a second.

Violet added, "Most people would label me as a high-functioning autistic, but I think we're all somewhere on the spectrum; it's just a case of where? Everyone only pays attention to those on the extreme, but even you exist somewhere on the spectrum. Where you are determines, generally speaking, how you live your life and how people perceive you. I don't consider myself 'high functioning,' though I understand why some people do because they compare me to other people they know and think that I'm doing better than them. It's not a fair comparison because everyone is different, and I have access to treatment most people don't."

"So," I asked tentatively, "when you say you 'tested in ways that they had never seen,' what does that mean?"

Violet looked directly at me in that way that made me feel like I was being completely heard. It was both an amazing gift and also a bit disconcerting. At least, it had been for me at first, but I found that the more time we spent together, the more I was getting used to it.

"First," she began, "as the concept of neurodiversity has become more mainstream, you need to understand that conditions like mine, or dyslexia, ADHD, et cetera are becoming more and more regarded as simple variations of the norm.

"In 2007, a YouTube video of Mel Baggs captured the way they read a book. They pressed their faces into the book, hummed to themselves, bobbed a Slinky up and down. Things that would seem abnormal to most neurotypical people. When Mel was interviewed, they explained they were trying to show the joy of their world. They talked about the way they move as a response to everything that is going on around them. As Mel put it, they were in a constant conversation with every aspect of their environment."

Violet paused briefly before continuing, "I'm sure you've probably seen videos of autistic people who can paint amazing pictures, or even seemingly neurotypical people who can paint with both hands and feet at the same time?"

I nodded. I remembered seeing a post on social media about both types of people.

"These are just 'normal' people"—she used air quotes for emphasis—"who fall on the spectrum. We notice them because they can do something most people can't, and thus we label them autistic or on the edge of the spectrum or whatever, but the fact is there are people like that all around us. Neuroscientists are identifying spectrum signs from everyone from Bill Gates to Einstein and everyone in between. The point is, it's not about who is on the spectrum but where we all fall on it.

"As for me, my brain is just wired differently than yours or most people, even those on the edges of the spectrum. I see and hear and smell everything all the time. My brain is a little like the new AI engines that thirst for information. My brain does that too. It is constantly looking for data to absorb."

"That must be exhausting."

Violet smiled wistfully. "It is. There was a time when my body would literally shut down from exhaustion. But now, I'm on a cocktail of drugs that help me process the data without it overwhelming my body. It's more complicated than that, but I don't want to bore you."

"You're not boring me." The words came out before I could stop them, and I felt myself blush.

We talked for a while longer as I kept asking for more detail on how her brain worked, what it felt like, how she dealt with all the information. I was fascinated by it, and it helped explain a lot about some of her quirky mannerisms. Eventually, we got back to work, and then it was time to take our second sleep of the trip.

———— • ⧈ • ————

Violet couldn't fall back asleep. Aside from all the work talk they had spent most of the day discussing, she couldn't stop thinking about the earlier part of their conversation.

No one had ever asked much about who she was or her past before. Certainly, no one had ever paid as close attention as Ethan had as she tried to explain how her brain worked. She had always been afraid that trying to explain herself would simply scare people away, but the more she talked, the more he wanted to know. He seemed genuinely interested in who she was, not just what she knew or how she could help him. That was new. At least that was what her computer brain was reporting back after its perfunctory analysis of everything they had discussed.

As she lay with her eyes open, trying to go through the sleeping routine that her multiple therapists had developed to help her shut down her brain enough to rest, she stared at the airplane ceiling and felt herself smiling again.

Chapter 12
City in a Garden

Eventually, we landed at Changi Airport, made our way through customs, and collected our baggage. Before we left, Violet insisted on taking me to see the Jewel Changi Rain Vortex, a forty-meter-high indoor waterfall. While on the plane, I had read in the brochure that it was surrounded by over two thousand trees and many tropical plants. I'd never seen anything like it anywhere, and certainly not in an airport.

As I walked into this forest within the airport and saw the incredible architecture of the circular waterfall, I thought, *No wonder Singapore is known as a "City in a Garden."*

As we got into a taxi to head to our hotel, Violet said, "The reason I wanted you to come here is to meet Meiying Li. She is one of the people responsible for the transformation of Singapore's new identity and cultural movement. Technically, she's Singapore's director of tourism, but it's so much more."

"OK," I said, "but why halfway across the world? Wasn't there someone closer?"

"Ethan," Violet said, looking at me briefly before glancing out the car window and back again as she always did, "the people I'm having you meet are vastly different from one another. They come from different backgrounds and work in completely different industries. Meiying doesn't just work for a company; she works for the entire city, if not the whole of Singapore."

She didn't explain further, and I spent the rest of the taxi ride trying to let that sink in.

We had plenty of time before our meeting. I took a long, hot shower, trying to unwind my aching muscles from the long flight, and then I lay down for a quick nap. Although it was getting close to lunchtime locally, the time zone changes and the flight had my body all out of sorts, and I needed rest more than food.

I woke up to hear a phone ringing. Disoriented, I surveyed my surroundings. I had been so deeply asleep that it took a few moments for me to remember where I was. I found the source of the ringing and picked up the receiver of the phone by my bed.

"Hello," I said, my voice sounding frog-like.

"I thought we might want to eat something before we see Meiying," Violet said into my ear. She sounded wide awake.

"Umm," I said, my brain still trying to spin awake. "Yeah, sure."

"Great, I'll meet you in the lobby in ten minutes."

I was about to suggest perhaps a little longer, but the line was dead.

I found Violet sitting on a luxurious-looking sofa in the lobby, her head darting this way and that, taking in everything that was happening—and there was a lot happening. There seemed to be some kind of convention going on, and in addition to all the people with various name badges hanging from lanyards around their necks, there was a troupe of dancers in brightly colored flowing garments performing acrobatic dances in the middle of the lobby.

It looked like something you might see from street buskers in many places around the world, but here, this was just Singapore being Singapore.

I stopped and just stared at Violet, watching her expression as she looked around the room. To most people it might seem like her expression wasn't changing at all, but I read her signs as though they were the tell of a poker player. Her eyes would squint just a bit if she saw something interesting. Just a fleeting moment, and then they were back to normal. Her nostrils might flare slightly, or her head would pause on its swivel for a second, no longer, before continuing its journey.

As her gaze continued along its path, her eyes finally settled on me, and her face lit up for a brief moment. She smiled. I felt like a summer breeze had come in through the door, light and airy and full of the scent of flowers. Then she stood up and began walking toward me.

I knew I was probably smiling too much myself, but I didn't care. "Did you get any rest?" I asked as we met behind the crowd watching the dancers.

She thought for a moment. "Yes. You?"

I laughed. "Yeah, if you hadn't called, I might not have woken up."

"There's a great little restaurant here in the hotel," she said, and led the way as if I hadn't said anything. I chuckled to myself and followed her.

Violet was watching Ethan closely throughout their dinner. The place was typical of hotel restaurants and catered to the family and business clientele that made up the bulk of the hotel's business.

She took in all the various sounds, sights, and especially the smells from the various foods being served from the kitchen. One thing she enjoyed most when she traveled was having new experiences, regardless of which senses she was using, but food and the aroma of new spices or combinations of food had always been among her favorite things.

They spent some time just talking about the history of Singapore and especially Meiying's role. Violet told him how the two had met and some things she had done to help Meiying when she was just getting started.

"Meiying, by the way, means 'beautiful flower,' which, as you will see, fits her perfectly."

Ethan had smiled then and turned the conversation back to Violet, asking, "How do you handle all the information coming at you? I mean, is it difficult to process that much information? Do you even know it's happening?"

He seemed, as before, to be genuinely interested, so she answered him.

"I'm no different from someone who has a skill, like artists or musicians. In fact, I really love music. It's one of the things that I feel the most." She pinched her thumb and fingers together when she said the word, attempting to show him what she meant. "The doctors first thought I had a particular type of photographic memory, which I guess wasn't too far off, but I'm not like other people who have that type of memory. My brain does things a little differently."

"What do you mean?" Ethan asked.

Here Violet paused. She knew exactly what she meant but had always struggled to articulate it. "The closest thing I can think of that may make sense to you is that instead of a photo in my mind that I can look at and recall, it's more like a database. Folders, files, all sorted and compartmentalized. Things get ordered, even numbered, and I can find them *whenever I want. It's like a large catalog of data I can sort and reorder however I want."*

Ethan leaned his elbows on the table. "So," he began, "how long do you store the data?"

Violet scrunched her face a little. "It's difficult to explain, but basically, for as long as I think I need to."

"How do you retrieve the information?"

Violet laughed a little. "I just ask for it or find the answer to a question someone else asks." She could see Ethan frowning. "Jeffery and I used to play a game." She was looking directly at Ethan now. "He would look around the room and ask me about something or someone." Then she added, "As long as it's not someone who just walked in and I haven't seen them."

She watched as Ethan scanned the room, then he said, "There's a family with three kids. One is in a high chair."

Without even thinking about it, Violet described them in very minute detail. The color of the children's socks, the bows in the girl's hair, the outfits each person was wearing, even the color of the buttons on the man's shirt and the eyes of the stuffed animal one child was holding.

She saw Ethan's jaw drop. She hadn't been trying to show off, and it hadn't occurred to her it might come across that way. One of the biggest challenges she faced, the doctors had told her, was her difficulty with social graces. She understood the concept of them, just not the when and how of them. So, when someone asked her a question like this, she did her best to answer, not realizing that it could come across a certain way.

Ethan, however, didn't seem to mind. "That's incredible."

Violet shrugged as she instinctively began looking around the room again. "It's just how my brain works. I can tell you just about what everyone is eating right now. I can even tell you the songs, in order, that have been playing over the speakers from the moment we walked in up to now."

"Really?"

He seemed skeptical, so she told him. He just sat back and half laughed. "That's crazy."

Violet focused on him intensely, trying to determine whether he was put off by her recall ability. Just as she was trying to make a determination, he leaned forward and began asking her even more questions. Not about what she could do, but how it felt, if she was ever afraid or nervous. He took an actual interest in her as a person and how her brain affected her.

No one had ever asked so many questions about her. It was simultaneously interesting and refreshing. Once again, she had the unfamiliar experience of catching herself smiling.

Chapter 13
Meiying

The sun had just set as we arrived at the Gardens by the Bay. The first thing I noticed—they were hard to miss—were the "Supertrees." These giant, man-made structures with plants growing up the side were clearly made of steel or wire. Their size and the adorning plants were something to behold.

I'm sure I stood out as the typical tourist with my mouth wide open as our taxi dropped us off. I was still looking up more than where I was going, so it wasn't until I heard someone say Violet's name that my attention turned earthbound.

"It is so good to see you," Violet said, hugging an Asian woman of medium height. She had long, jet-black hair and wore an electric-blue dress with black flower patterns.

"I am so happy to see *you*," the woman answered, emphasizing the last word.

"Meiying Li," Violet said, dropping one of her arms and gesturing toward me, "may I present Ethan Knight."

Meiying had bright brown eyes, and she smiled widely as she held out her hand. "It is nice to meet you," she said as I took it. Her accent was Asian, though there was a hint of what sounded like a British lilt to her voice. "Please call me Mei."

I smiled back. "It's a pleasure to meet you as well. Please call me Ethan."

"OK," Violet said, "I will see you both later." She turned back to Meiying; they hugged again and kissed each other on the cheek, and just like that I was standing alone yet again with someone I had just met.

Stretching out her arm, Meiying indicated what looked like a fancy golf cart but without the room for golf bags on the back. The cart came with a driver in a uniform, who was sitting in front. There were plenty of open-sided shuttle buses scattered around, and this looked like a mini version with just two rows of seats.

"This way," she said, and led us to the cart. We sat next to each other in the back, and the driver whisked us away after handing two lanyards to us.

I looked at mine; it had today's date and "VIP" on the front.

"Do you know anything about the gardens?" Meiying asked.

"No."

"I fear this may not be the best place to have our training, as it can be quite distracting," she said, and I knew what she meant. I was already getting sidetracked as we drove by amazing displays of horticulture, and I wasn't even a "garden guy." Meiying continued, "However, no trip to Singapore would be complete without visiting them. I know Violet says you have little time, and so we will have the short version of the tour if that is all right with you."

I looked back at her smiling face. "It's perfectly fine. It's very kind of you to take the time to do this, and I promise to pay close attention to the training."

She smiled back and let me enjoy the ride as we passed by the Supertrees, somewhat to my disappointment, and stopped in front of a massive glass dome. It formed a huge snake-like tube that emerged from the ground and went back into it. The sign read appropriately, "Flower Dome."

As we walked past all the people standing in line and entered the massive structure via special access for "VIP ONLY," Meiling said, "Another reason I wanted to bring you here has to do with the sixth Pillar of Humanagement, as well as the identity of Singapore."

I was not ready for what I saw as we entered the dome. With the sun outside beginning to set, lights were turning on inside, illuminating plants and trees and all manner of vegetation, the likes of which I had never seen before.

"Over three thousand glass panels with over forty different shapes and sizes are used to cover the dome," Meiying said, sounding like a tour guide. "In 2015, the Guinness Book of World Records labeled this the largest glass greenhouse in the world."

I just shook my head. "I believe it," I said as we began walking down a path, along with several groups of tourists doing the same thing.

Remembering my promise to stay focused, I turned to her and asked, "So what is the sixth Pillar and how does it relate to all this and Singapore's identity?"

"You have heard of our brand, our motto?" she asked. "Passion Made Possible?"

I nodded. I had read a little on the plane and knew the city had rebranded in 2017.

"The sixth Pillar follows the acronym COP." She pronounced each letter.

Violet sure loved her acronyms. "Violet named the sixth Pillar after the police?" I said, looking at Meiying and smiling.

She laughed a little. "No. It has nothing to do with that term."

We waited as a gaggle of young schoolchildren raced past us, screaming at the top of their lungs in a language I couldn't understand, before she continued, "The letters stand for Culture of Purpose, but here in Singapore we prefer to use Culture of Passion." She beamed.

I nodded. I could see how the two might be intertwined.

"How much do you know about the concept of tribes?"

"A little," I said truthfully. "I watched that one marketing guy's TED Talk about it. I think he wrote a book too."

Meiying continued walking. "Yes, Seth Godin. His work on the subject is probably the best-known, and his book called *Tribes* introduced many people to this notion. There is another book called *Tribal Leadership*, which was written by three researchers: Dave Logan, John King, and Halee Fischer-Wright. This book looks at tribes from a business standpoint."

As we walked, my eyes kept getting drawn to the intricate displays woven into the incredible plants and flowers. We passed Mother Hubbard's shoe, an Eiffel Tower climbing with plants, large insect sculptures, and even a row of wooden elephants.

"There are many concepts of tribes, and each is valuable," Meiying said. "However, in our Culture of Passion, we focus more on the notion of a family than a tribe. I'll explain more in a few minutes.

"First, let us examine what a Culture of Passion or Purpose is. It is both a mindset and an acknowledgment that our work and our life do not have to be separate."

"OK," I said. "You've got my attention; tell me more."

"The idea is simple. Help people find the passion or purpose in the work that they do."

"Yeah, I've heard that before," I said, "and I get it, but sometimes people work just to, you know, pay the bills. We can't all be passionate about what we do."

"Why not?" She asked, looking at me with a serious expression.

"Well," I stammered, thrown off a little by her intense gaze. "Like I said, sometimes people work because they're good at something or because it's what they know how to do, not necessarily because it's their lifelong passion. They just need to make a living."

"What you say is true, but you are making the mistake of confusing someone's passion or purpose with the work that they do," she answered matter-of-factly.

Now I was confused. "Huh?"

"In the book *Tribal Leadership*, the authors talked about a company that was in the biotech industry. A very successful and growing company . The researchers asked the employees one question: Who are your competitors? What do you think their answer was?"

I thought about it for a few seconds. "I suppose some of the larger biotech companies, maybe a big pharma company, or even a large healthcare conglomerate?"

"Yes, that would be the expected answer," she said, "but that was not the answer they received. The employees' answer to the question of who they were competing against was this: We are in competition with cancer."

I stopped walking and looked at her. "Whoa!" I said, impressed.

Meiying nodded and motioned for us to continue walking amid the lush green foliage in the warm, humid air. "Yes. I, too, had a similar reaction when I heard this. Clearly, this is a company with a Culture of Purpose, if not a true Culture of Passion.

"But you see, this has nothing to do with the labor of their job, their function, their . . . how did you put it? The thing they are good at?"

I nodded my head slowly, my brain wrapping itself once again around a concept I had never considered before.

"When we can find passion for why we are doing what we do, not just what it is we do, we see our work in a different light," she said. "When you combine this with how different people are approaching work in today's society, it becomes more important than ever to find that passion, that purpose in the work that we do."

As I stared at the enormous glass dome we were walking beneath, I realized how each of these Pillars Violet created did indeed build upon each other, just as the glass pieces fit together like a jigsaw puzzle to form the canopy.

We had reached the exit of the Flower Dome, and we climbed into our waiting cart for a quick ride toward the Supertrees. The sky was darkening now, and the trees were lit with an array of colored lights. People were sitting on the grass; some had brought blankets, and a huge TV screen acted like a stage as the lights performed a show all around us. Music blended with lights, creating a surreal and magnificent experience in the early night.

We stopped, and I got out of the cart, just looking up into the canopy of these not-quite-artificial trees with their incredible display of changing lights and hearing the music soaring through loudspeakers. It was truly breathtaking to be a part of.

After some time, Meiying (having kept quiet to allow me to enjoy the wonder of these iconic giant trees) told me we should keep moving. There was a huge observatory platform that connected many of the trees and that visitors could go up and walk on. Given that they were easily fifty or sixty feet in the air, and I am not a fan of heights, I was glad we weren't heading in that direction.

Instead, we turned back the way we had come, and this time headed to the second monolithic glass dome. This one had a sign that read "Cloud Forest."

Chapter 14
The Sixth Pillar

Continuing as if we hadn't ever stopped talking, Meiying said, "The challenge is getting employees to buy in. When a company is started, it is often named after the person who started it. This simple act, naming a company, can just by itself alienate people from feeling connected. After all, how does one 'buy in' or 'take ownership' of something when the very name of the organization is about someone else? It means nothing to them, so how can they be emotionally connected?"

Perhaps sensing my confusion, she continued explaining as we walked into the second glass dome and a whole different world with a mountain, trees, even a huge waterfall. "The point is, Ethan, that a Culture of Passion and Purpose is so much more than simply finding joy in your work. You will cover some of that in the final Pillar.

"Passion, and one's purpose at work, is something that exists beyond the individual. It is a two-way street that encompasses both how the employee brings passion to what they do and how the employer builds a culture that fosters passion and purpose."

We began ascending a walkway called Treetop Walk, and while I wasn't crazy about the idea of going "up," I was mostly focused on what Meiying was teaching me and didn't really pay attention. "So how do you get this Culture of Passion working?" I asked.

"There are many ways. First, you must invest in your employees if you hope to have them invest in you or your company."

"What do you mean?"

"It can be something simple, like helping them explore new paths of education, but it can also be more fundamental," she said. "Like investing time in what they care about. Giving them the freedom and support to tie their passion to their work. For example, if someone is in the financial department of a company, you might allow them time to teach one class a week at a local school on the basics of finance. This connects what they do at work with something outside of their work. Another is what we like to call passion projects."

We were climbing higher and higher, literally now walking among the treetops. Although I got a little unsettled if I looked straight down, I was mostly surveying what was all around me from a point of view I normally would never have. I also stayed in the middle of the walk, which was solid, as opposed to the grating on either side.

Looking over at Meiying and smiling nervously, I said, "What are passion projects?"

"We allow our employees to take half of one day each week to work on a project they are passion about."

"What do you mean, like they can do anything they want?" I asked.

"Yes and no. They must present the idea first and report on the outcome when it is complete, but otherwise they are free to work on anything."

"What does 'presenting an idea' mean?"

"For example, someone in a sales department might want to try creating an outreach program, perhaps helping members of the community as a way of showing how the company and individuals care about the community in which they sell."

"So, it's like volunteering," I said.

"Yes, it can be. It might also be someone from engineering wanting to work on creating a robot which has nothing to do with their normal engineering work or the work the company needs, but it is a creative expression of their passion."

"Wait," I said, stopping and turning to face her, "you mean they waste half a day a week working on something that is basically a hobby for them? How does that help the company?"

Turning to keep us moving, she smiled and said, "In terms of traditional productivity measurement, yes, I suppose you might say that those hours are not spent doing productive work that results in something measurable for the company.

"However, what is immeasurable is the creativity that such an activity enables." She looked over to make sure I had heard her, then went on to explain, "The time taken to explore a hobby, as you call it, or to work outside the company on another project, does not relate one-to-one in an exchange for productivity at the company. What it does is allow the employee an outlet for their creativity or engagement. This outlet allows them to rejuvenate, to break from the normal hours spent at their job. Very often, a solution to a problem they are struggling with suddenly comes to mind following their passion project time.

"Also, employees are more productive going into and coming out of the time they spend working on their passion project, as it invigorates them. Knowing that the company will invest this time in them helps them feel more connected to the company, and thus they work harder."

Having arrived in the middle of the mountain full of plants, we now ascended a series of escalators to what the signs referred to as the Cloud Walk. The higher we rose, the more nervous I became and the more intently I focused on our discussion.

"Shouldn't employees be at work to, well, do work though?" I asked.

"Of course—there is no hard and fast rule about how this works, Ethan. The leaders at each company must decide for themselves how they will implement their Culture of Passion and how each employee will fit into it.

"Another consideration is finding that overarching Culture of Passion and Purpose for the company. Some call it a noble purpose. The notion that there is something bigger than the company to work for."

"Like the employees who said their competition was cancer?"

"Yes," Meiying answered, "but it doesn't have to be that specific. For some, it is giving back to communities, doing less harm to the planet, and being part of an industry-wide solution to a global problem. It can be anything that excites and bonds employees together. Something to unite the tribe."

We had reached the top, and while the view was indeed breathtaking, I was frozen. The walkway stretched out over the expanse below, and although it was held up with steel beams, every nerve in my body was on edge. It was also incredibly warm in this indoor tropical forest, and I was sweating even more now.

Meiying asked if I was OK. She told me we did not have to go on the walk if I didn't want to. The view was too hard to pass up, so I told her I'd be OK if I stayed in the middle of the walk.

"Which brings me back to family," she said as we took our first few tentative steps onto the Cloud Walk above the treetops. "We have found that when one takes the concept of tribes and turns it into the notion of family, the passion and purpose are far more easily found."

"What do you mean by family?"

She answered my question with one of her own: "When you think of being part of a workforce, how does that differ from being part of a family?"

She paused but didn't quite wait for me to answer. "When an organization treats people as if they belong to one big family, it changes the way they behave on both sides. Both the employer and employee approach what they do and how they do it differently.

"There is a genuine caring about everyone as individuals and about the company as a whole. When a Culture of Passion is part of a family, everyone is working toward the same goals of supporting each other, bringing out the best in each other, ensuring that everyone's needs are met at every level. Can you now see the outcome of such a culture?" She asked, turning to me and flashing her smile once more.

I had to smile myself as more of the pieces fell into place. "Yes," I said, nodding. "I imagine the outcome is better productivity."

She nodded like a teacher appreciating a student's understanding of the lesson. We were at a hairpin turn on the walk, which now overlooked a great swath of the forest below. With a little encouragement, she got me to walk to the railing. Hanging on with white knuckles, I looked out over the expanse below. I could even see the first section of the path quite a way down, which at the time had seemed high. Misting jets created a cloudlike atmosphere. Even in my heightened state of fear, I could still appreciate the beauty of this unique vantage point.

Trying not to focus on the idea of falling from such a height, I asked, "I've heard that some people don't like the idea of an employer being a family because they feel like work is work and family is family and the two should not mix."

Meiying nodded. "Yes, I too have heard these complaints. Usually, however, this is because there is no Culture of Purpose or Passion. There is only work. There is only productivity."

As we turned to continue our journey, Meiying faced me and said, "It is important to remember that although increased productivity is one outcome, it is not the goal."

I nodded, knowing that where we were heading was likely the most important lesson of all.

We made our way back to the mountain and then down a cool, winding path behind six large waterfalls. Soon, we were back on the ground at a sign that read "Waterfall View." Looking up at the six long streams of water, I felt almost overwhelmed at the enormity of what I was trying to do.

Perhaps sensing my dilemma, or perhaps because of the shortened time frame Violet had told Meiying we were under, she said without looking at me, "Violet's program, HABBIT21, is not something you can accomplish overnight, Ethan. It takes time. Each component must stand on its own before you can build the next.

"Each one, however, will have an immediate impact on your Culture of Passion. Each Pillar will lay the foundation that can completely transform your business and the lives of those who work with you."

She turned toward me, her voice softening a little. "What you are doing is difficult, Ethan, but it is important work.

The change you are seeking will take time, effort, and a lot of trust. What you will have at the end may or may not look like what you expect, but it will transform you and those around you."

Suddenly Violet walked up to us, out of nowhere.

Meiying smiled broadly. "Did you get some good photos?"

Violet looked at her phone, scrolling up rapidly with her finger. "Let's see . . . seven hundred and ninety-two," she proclaimed proudly.

I raised my eyebrows. "Wait, you've been here taking photos this whole time?"

Violet looked at me with that blank expression that was either disdain, boredom, or simply recognition. "Yes, and there's one of your face before you stepped out onto the Cloud Walk that is priceless."

Looking back and forth between them, I could tell from their smiles that I was the only one who hadn't been in on their little secret.

Violet, her head remaining uncharacteristically still, looked back at me and said, "I knew you would want to take photos while you were walking and couldn't, so I took them for you. I'll upload them tonight so you can see."

Despite my flush of embarrassment, I was touched by her thoughtfulness.

Meiying said she was sorry it was so late, as there was so much more to see in the gardens, but she knew our timeline was tight and the park was closing soon.

We pulled up to the entrance of the park in our little golf cart. This time Meiying had sat in front with the driver. When we stopped, the two women said goodbye with a warm embrace. Meiying offered me a hug as well and gave me a long, heartfelt squeeze.

"Ethan, it was so very nice to meet you," she said as she pulled away. "If there is anything I can do to help you, all you have to do is ask. I also hope you will come back one day when you have more time. I would be happy to show you more of the gardens and of our beautiful city."

"Thank you," I said. "I'd like that."

"One last thing," she said, motioning toward Violet. "One reason we wanted you to come here is because these gardens are where passion comes alive. Although this place's purpose is to highlight a city within a garden, I believe it also highlights the incredible creativity of its designers and is a living, breathing example of a Culture of Passion.

"Bringing this Pillar to life in your own business, community, and life will take a great deal of creativity. I hope that when you need a spark of creativity, you will think of this magical place and it will help you in some way."

I couldn't think of a more appropriate synergy between the gardens and the Pillar.

Chapter 15
The SkyBridge

*V*iolet got into the taxi next to Ethan. She pulled up the photos she had been taking and showed him the one she had alluded to, from before he stepped out onto the Cloud Walk. The look on his face was one of pure terror.

Ethan laughed. She noticed the way his dimples deepened when he smiled, and she immediately realized why that thought had occurred to her. It was quickly replaced with a myriad of other thoughts about all the things going on around her.

Refocusing, she said, "The Cloud Walk is only thirty-five meters high."

He laughed. "Oh, only thirty-five meters . . . you know, roughly a football field."

"What are you so scared of?" Violet asked. "The walk is made of steel; it's not going to break."

She could see anxiety written all over his face as he thought about it.

"Uh-huh" was all he could manage to say.

"You know," Violet continued, curious about this reaction, "over fifty million people have visited the gardens since it opened, and a lot of them have walked the Cloud Walk. It's really safe."

Ethan answered quickly, "After all this time, I'd hate to have been the one guy who breaks the safety record."

"You're a pretty logical guy, Ethan," Violet said, turning to look at him in the back seat of the taxi. "I don't understand why this bothers you."

"It has nothing to do with logic," he said. "I don't think about how the walk is made, or the strength and thickness of the steel. When I look over the edge, it's a feeling that takes over my entire body. I can't explain it, but when I get close to an edge like that, my heart races, I start to sweat, I can't breathe." He shook his body, clearly trying to get rid of the feelings. "It's the way it feels, not the way I think."

Violet didn't say anything. She felt like a little girl who had just figured out a problem. She had never understood why people with phobias acted the way they did. It didn't make sense to be afraid of something you could explain away with science or facts. She had tried reading about phobias and watching documentaries, but it never clicked—until now.

The way Ethan had said it—"It's the way it feels, not the way I think"—had suddenly allowed the last piece of the puzzle to fall into place for her. It made sense now, and she smiled happily as they climbed out of the taxi in front of their hotel. Another cog had slipped into its slot in the wheel of complexity that was Ethan Knight.

As they approached the hotel entrance, Ethan seemed nervous. Suddenly he said, "I was thinking of taking a walk down the waterfront promenade." Then, after an awkward pause, he added, "Do you want to come with me?"

Although Violet had to be up early, she knew she wouldn't be asleep for a few more hours. Besides, the night was pleasant, with a warm breeze. She agreed, and they set off among the multi-colored jets of water fountains and the bright lights of the city.

There were people walking everywhere—crowds of tourists with guides, families with strollers, and many street merchants vying for their trade. Violet's senses were on overdrive, taking everything in.

There were times when so much sensation made her want to run away and hide. Other times, she reveled in it. This felt somewhat different. She felt calmer than normal, walking with Ethan among the lights and sounds and smells, among the throngs of people, the snippets of conversations in multiple languages, the music and sounds of the city.

Her brain still registered and cataloged what she saw, but it wasn't starved for information like it often was when she craved distractions. Nor was it feeling overwhelmed or burdened by the massive amount of input.

Instead, she took on what she wanted and—to her surprise—she could ignore what she didn't. On some level, she felt like this happened all the time, but it was the first time she had recognized the difference. When she was around Ethan, she didn't have to work at filtering the information; it was happening in the background, and her focus was on him. That was new.

Interesting.

Ethan was talking about some of what Meiying had been teaching him, and she fielded his questions, discussing tactics on how he might implement the next phases of Humanagement into his company.

They stopped for some ice cream from a food truck and laughed when they both simultaneously ordered the same flavor: coffee ice cream with chocolate and caramel sauce.

He asked her how long she had known Meiying. After she told him, he said, "And part of her job is being in charge of the gardens?"

Violet smiled. "No. Actually, she is the executive creative director of the Singapore Tourism Board."

Ethan whistled and smiled, impressed. "Wow, you sure know some interesting people."

Violet nodded and thought, You're one of them. She looked out over the water so he wouldn't see the frown on her face as she wrestled with why that thought had jumped out at her.

Time seemed to stand still as they walked along the waterfront and outskirts of the city and then back to their hotel. But as they entered the lobby, Violet noticed that the clock behind the reception desk showed it was nearly midnight.

They had rooms in different towers of the hotel, but without thinking, Violet got into Ethan's elevator and pushed the button for the SkyBridge that connected the towers.

"Thanks for going on the walk," Ethan said, his voice oddly strained.

"It was fun," she said, wondering if the people on the elevator understood English or if they could sense the awkwardness that suddenly filled the small space.

As the door to the SkyBridge opened, they saw a large group of revelers dancing and playing music from some phone speakers in the middle of the expansive connection between the towers. The group was young and loud and just having fun. Violet said, "Goodnight," and exited the elevator. After a few steps, she looked over her shoulder and waved.

She turned, then halted. Ethan had jumped out of the elevator just as the doors closed.

My heart was pounding in my chest. It was like I remember feeling when I was at a middle school dance, unsure of what to do, afraid of what she might do. She stood there looking at me with a slight frown, her eyes darting quickly left and right but always coming back to my face.

I had to be losing my mind.

Why did I get off the elevator? Now I had to say something, and I had no idea what. I walked up and stood in front of her. The group of partygoers looked over and yelled something in Chinese that was probably an invitation to join them, but I was too panicked to look at them, much less take them up on their offer.

It was now or never. She opened her mouth to say something, and I leaned in. Not quickly—I didn't want to scare her—but deliberately. I was a couple of inches from her face. Her frown disappeared, and for a moment I thought she looked frightened, but then that too vanished, and she seemed uncertain of what expression to wear.

Her eyes were moving in double time now—far left, left, center, right, far right and back again.

If I didn't do it now, I would never get the nerve up again. I closed the gap between us and pressed my lips gently onto hers.

She didn't pull away. She didn't exactly kiss me back either. She just sort of stayed still.

I closed my eyes, desperately willing my body not to shake on the outside as much as I could feel myself shaking on the inside.

Her lips were warm and soft, slightly moist, and tasted a little of raspberries. Probably some type of lip balm. All this flashed through my mind in microseconds.

I didn't want to stop, but I opened my eyes and gently pulled back.

Her eyes were wide open. Had she even closed them? They were moving from side to side, not wide like before. She was looking rapidly from my left eye to my right eye and back again. I noticed her breathing was faster than it had been a moment ago.

I didn't know what to do. I was terrified. Even more than I had been standing on the Cloud Walk. *Should I say something? Was she angry? Did she like it?*

She turned her head and looked off to the right. Then she turned back and looked to the left, pausing ever so briefly to look me in the eye as her glance passed by me.

Then she gazed at the partygoers, and then out the glass windows of the SkyBridge.

Although the music from the dancers was loud, the silence between us was so awkward that I thought she must be able to hear my heart about to pound its way out of my chest.

"Um, well," I began, my throat dry, "I'd better get to sleep. Goodnight then."

"Yes," she answered much too quickly. "Goodnight."

And with that she turned and walked down toward the group of revelers, and I went to press the button for the elevator.

———————— · ⧞ · ————————

Violet walked toward, and then through, the group of young dancers, all gyrating and bouncing to the music that blared around them. They parted to let her through, gesturing and urging her in Mandarin to stop and join them. A few of the young girls held out a bottle of alcohol to her as she passed.

Violet just kept walking. She barely registered any of it.

Her mind was in chaos. Like an explosion in space where there is no oxygen for fuel, quick flashes of light that burn bright white and then suddenly extinguish.

She just couldn't understand it.

When she had stepped off the elevator, her eyes had quickly taken in every facet of what was happening on the SkyBridge.

The sounds of the music, the laughter, and the screams. She knew there were seventeen people, ten men and seven women. She knew what each of them was wearing, down to the women's earrings and the men's belt buckles. She knew they were mostly in their twenties. She understood snippets of what they were saying in Mandarin. She knew they were asking her to come and join them. She could even see the silver water of the bay out one side of the windows and the lights of the city skyscrapers out the other.

Then she had turned to wave goodnight, and Ethan had stepped out of the elevator. She hadn't expected that, nor had she been prepared for his kiss, but none of that was what now consumed and confounded her overactive brain.

In fact, that was the very thing she was confused about. Her overactive brain.

The moment Ethan had kissed her, everything had stopped. Everything.

The sounds, the sights, everything that was going on around her had gone silent. She had watched almost in slow motion as he closed his eyes. She had taken in his gentle lips, the slight scent of his cologne, but even those things were mostly afterthoughts.

As long as his lips touched hers, she was completely and utterly calm. No fireworks of thoughts, no flashes of light, no constant stream of data input. Everything in her mind had gone silent. She had been unable to move, to react, to respond in any way. Not because she hadn't wanted to, but because she was so shocked.

This . . . nothingness . . . *had never happened to her before.*

Chapter 16
Breakfast

I didn't sleep much.

What had I been thinking?

It must have been jet lag. That's what I tried to tell myself as I justified being so dumb. She had seemed so shocked when I stopped kissing her. She had clearly not wanted to kiss me back.

Now I was supposed to meet Violet for breakfast in the hotel restaurant before she left for a meeting, and then we were heading back to the airport for the next leg of our trip to Sweden. Not only would I have to face her for breakfast, but then we'd have an over sixteen-hour flight together.

Chastising myself, I got up, showered, and dressed, and with the proverbial tail between my legs I headed down to the restaurant.

The hostess told me my "guest" was already seated and led me to her table. As we approached, Violet was on her cell phone.

"Uhm . . ." she said into the phone. "I'm with a . . . client."

There was a pause while she listened to the response.

Seemingly surprised, she raised her eyebrows and asked, "Do I?"

Another pause followed by, "OK, I'd better get going. Thanks for calling. Give my love to Mary. Goodbye, Oliver."

Putting the phone away, she looked up and said, "Sorry about that."

I waved my hand to signal 'No problem' and studied the menu. Violet began looking around the way she always did.

Needing something to say, I said, "Do you what?"

Violet, whose gaze had already wandered around the room twice, cocked her head slightly and said, "What?"

"Your call," I said, gesturing to her phone. "Just now, on the phone, you said, 'Do I?'" I put down my menu, then added, "I was just curious what it was about. If it's none of my business, I apologize."

The server chose that moment to put me out of my misery and arrived to ask about our order, so we rescanned the menus and gave him our choices.

Once he had left, Violet asked what I thought about my time with Meiying yesterday.

I took a breath, glad she hadn't brought up my awkward attempt at kissing her and grateful that she wanted to move on. *Fine by me. Let's just get back to business.*

We talked more about the Culture of Passion and Purpose and went into detail about how I could implement various components of it and how soon. Despite the creative conversation and the passion with which Violet talked about it, I couldn't keep my mind from wandering back to what happened last night.

How could I have misjudged things so much? I thought, losing track of what Violet was saying. My mind just kept replaying that look in her eyes when we finished the kiss. Aside from that embarrassing moment, however, I also replayed the feel of her lips, the trembling I had felt, and the complete wonder of the moment. Of course, no matter how many times my mind replayed that part, it always ended with the embarrassing finish.

I tried to bring myself back to the present moment and saw that Violet was staring at me intently. *Uh oh.* Clearly, she had said something, expecting an answer, and I had not been paying attention. *Busted!*

"Sorry," I said, "my mind was somewhere else."

Violet cocked her head slightly, and her eyes narrowed. She said, "There's a lesson that gets passed around every few years or so." Then, she reached over and picked up her water glass.

Here we go, I thought to myself. *I'm going to get the 'Is this glass half full or half empty' talk.*

It seemed being wrong about Violet was becoming a habit for me.

She said, "A psychologist held up a glass of water to an audience and asked, 'How heavy is this glass of water?' People yelled out everything from eight ounces to twenty. Then someone yelled out that the water would have weight, so more answers followed, going as high as forty-five and fifty ounces.

"Once the audience had satisfied itself with guesses, the psychologist said, 'The weight of the glass doesn't matter. What is relevant is how long I hold it. If I lift it up and hold it for a minute, it's not a problem. If I hold it for fifteen minutes, I'll have an ache in my arm. If I try to hold it for several hours, my arm will feel numb and will become paralyzed. In each case, the weight of the glass doesn't change, but the longer I hold it, the heavier it becomes.'"

Violet looked back at me. "The psychologist then told the audience that the stresses and worries of life were like the glass of water. When we think about them for a little while, nothing much happens. But"—now Violet picked up her glass again—"if we think about them longer, they begin to hurt us. If we don't put them down, they can paralyze us."

With that, she put her glass back down and smiled at me.

I must have looked stupid staring at her with my mouth open, but I couldn't help it. Was she talking about last night? Was it that obvious how nervous I still was this morning?

Then she asked me the question she must have asked when I was daydreaming a minute ago. Thankfully, it was about my talk with Meiying, and we resumed talking about the Culture of Purpose as though this strange interaction, not to mention last night, never happened.

Eventually, we finished our breakfast, and we left the hotel together as the doorman hailed a cab with his whistle. Violet had a meeting she needed to attend before we left for the airport.

In what felt like a never-ending series of awkward moments, I wasn't sure what to do when the cab pulled up. I partially extended one arm while simultaneously half-opening the other, unsure whether to shake her hand, give her a hug, or just walk away in shame.

Violet leaned in for a hug.

I'm not sure why, but I kissed her gently on the cheek and then opened the door for her. She slipped inside and reached for the door handle to close the door. As she did, she looked up at me and said, "You sound funny."

I wasn't sure I had heard her correctly and pulled my head back a bit. Frowning, I said, "I sound funny? What do you mean?"

She looked up at me and said, "It's what Oliver said to me. When I asked him 'Do I?', then he said, 'Yes, you sound happy.'"

Then she closed the door, and the cab pulled away from the curb.

Violet turned in her seat and watched as a smile slowly spread across Ethan's face.

Smiling herself, she turned around and looked out the cab's window.

She could see that Ethan hadn't slept much, which gave them something in common. For all the "nothingness" his kiss had momentarily given her, the respite had been short-lived. As though wanting to punish her for this temporary reprieve, Violet's brain had gone into overdrive on the way back to her room.

The interesting thing was that it wasn't processing the usual myriads of information it collected all around her. Instead, her mind had focused on the minutest of details about the time she had spent with Ethan earlier, leading up to and including the moment of the kiss.

She replayed all the hundreds of photographs she had taken of him talking and walking with Meiying. So much so that she would bring each one up over the course of the night and analyze them one by one to see how they matched with her memory.

She listened to every word of their conversation on the way back to the hotel, the walk along the waterfront, the ice cream, and, of course, the elevator ride and the kiss. She spent most of the night replaying that interaction until she knew every nuance of what had happened.

She knew exactly how his eyes closed slowly as he leaned in to kiss her. She could recount precisely how he smelled, how his lips felt, how she had inhaled his scent slightly just as his lips met hers. She knew the exact count of eyelashes he had on both his upper eyelids. Less so on the bottom because she hadn't been able to see them as clearly.

She felt his slight shiver when their lips met and knew that her body had responded in kind.

Violet could have recounted with absolute accuracy how many seconds the kiss lasted and how long it took both of them to take a slow deep breath afterward, had it been videotaped for playback and verification.

Most important of all, however, she spent most of her time focusing on nothing. Specifically, the feeling of complete and utter calm that had come over her during the kiss. No "noise," no mental gymnastics. She couldn't explain it, couldn't understand the logic of it; she just lay there most of the time thinking about how amazing it felt.

Chapter 17
B.A.G.S.

Our next flight was another long one, and once again Violet had upgraded my ticket, so we were next to each other.

I was still walking with my feet off the ground after hearing her recount the phone conversation she'd had with her friend. Maybe I hadn't been so crazy after all.

Aside from getting some sleep, we spent a great deal of time reviewing what I had learned about HABBIT21 so far. Violet filled in some gaps that I hadn't had time to fully integrate on my crash course of her "future of work" model.

"Every company has baggage, or at least they should," she said at one point.

"What do you mean?" I asked.

"B.A.G.S.," she said, and I shook my head, smiling. Another acronym. "It stands for Being a Good Steward."

"I think that comes with the territory when you're a CEO," I said, "but I thought you said focusing on the bottom line *wasn't* what I should do?"

Violet looked over from her compartment seat and smiled. She opened her mouth to speak but then paused, our eyes locking briefly. As usual, I couldn't read her thoughts, but I realized her eyes weren't moving from side to side or moving at all for that matter. It seemed like a long time passed, but it was probably only a second or two. She blinked and then continued.

"That's because you're still stuck in your old habits of thinking only about revenue. When I say, 'being a good steward,' I am talking about much more than money."

Intrigued, I nodded for her to go on.

"What I'm about to say applies to businesses, and I mean all businesses. The culture of business has been so focused for so long on the bottom line that people have forgotten the role of business to begin with. It's only in recent years as the workforce has evolved that they, the workers, have reminded business about its true purpose."

I looked at her quizzically, and our eyes met again briefly. And again, she paused before resuming. "The true purpose of business is to find solutions to challenges. Put another way, to make things better."

I nodded. "OK," I said, "but what does that have to do with stewardship?"

"Everything," she answered. "When it's done correctly, a business doesn't just solve a problem, it makes things better." She could see I still didn't quite understand. "The problem is that companies have stopped at just solving the issue, and then they've focused on how to make more money doing it. Making things better, however, has to do with far more than simply solving a challenge.

"It's about making everything better. What I mean is that if you can solve a challenge, improve a community, maybe even give back to that community, take into consideration the impact your solution has on the planet, et cetera—*Now* you're beginning to make *all* things better, not just *one* thing."

I leaned my head back in my seat, digesting what she had said. Then I turned my head toward her. "Look, I'm all for doing the right thing, being good for the planet, et cetera, but sometimes doing what you're suggesting can cost a great deal of money. Retrofitting factories, or completely changing supply chains, which increases costs, and so on.

"Again, I think doing good is great, but at *some* point"—I threw up my hands for emphasis—"doesn't the bottom line have to play a role here?"

"Of course," she answered, taking me a little by surprise. "Businesses are in business after all to make money."

Finally, something I agreed with and that I already knew.

"What the people who run businesses don't understand is that doing good *is* good for the bottom line. It is possible to be a good steward and give back to the community or the environment and have it be profitable. Sir Richard Branson wrote a book called *Screw Business As Usual*, which is full of examples of businesses that have done just that. They have 'done good'"—she made air quotes—"and been more profitable."

At that moment, the flight attendants came by to serve dinner, and we took a break from talking business. As we were eating, I decided to change the conversation.

Violet was trying to quiet her brain's incessant need for information. Normally when she flew, she had her laptop full of videos and work that would keep her mind occupied until she was finally able to sleep.

Having Ethan next to her made that impossible. Even she knew that putting in her earbuds and working would be rude. Not that she minded the conversation. It was just that the flight was long, and with little new data to feed her mind, it was getting increasingly difficult to stay focused.

The flight attendant's interruption with dinner helped a little. Violet's mind, going through all the rituals and observations about each part of the food they were served, gave her a temporary respite.

Suddenly her mind recoiled, and she stopped with her fork halfway to her mouth.

She had to replay what Ethan had just said to make sure she had heard him correctly.

"Does it bother you when people stare at you?"

Most people never asked about her this way. Those who did (and who inevitably left once she gave them some insight into who she was) were simply another piece of data to absorb.

In the way that Violet's brain always did, she was processing these thoughts at lightning speed. What was it that frightened her about this question now? It took a few iterations of compiling and processing lots of data before she realized she didn't want Ethan to pull away.

She regarded him as he cut the food on his plate. Feeling anxious about how someone else reacted was completely new to her. She had anxiety in many forms, but they were always related to herself, not others. He turned and looked at her.

She saw his expression change, and he put his silverware down. "Look, I'm sorry. I didn't mean to intrude."

That wasn't how Violet's brain worked. There was no sense of intrusion. Without fully processing the way other people might, she simply started talking. "I don't think about it much, at least not anymore. I did when I was younger. It used to bother me a lot because I couldn't understand why."

"Makes sense."

"I spent a lot of time in social skills training classes, but each time the teacher or therapist would give up on me because I asked so many questions." Taking a quick breath, she added, *"That's probably why everyone leaves eventually."*

This time it was Ethan who stopped eating mid fork-to-mouth. His expression softened, *"What do you mean, everyone eventually?"*

Violet shrugged, *"I don't really have long relationships. Eventually, people get tired of,"* she paused, thinking of various ways to express the thought, then settled on, *"how I am."*

Looking over at Ethan, she saw him smile, but it was not a sarcastic expression—it was a genuine, full-on smile.

"I like to think of it as the Violet effect," he said, his eyes now smiling as much as his mouth.

Violet wasn't sure what he meant but looked away and said, *"Anyway, it's not just that. The energy it takes for my brain to do what it does takes a toll on me. At first—although I could compartmentalize things—because there was always a hunger for more and more, my mind got to a point where things got out of control."*

Ethan asked, *"What do you mean, 'out of control'?"*

Violet didn't look at him this time. *"Like I said before, I would eventually shut down, but before that I would have outbursts, uncontrollable fits, sometimes violent, sometimes just against myself. Sort of like epileptic fits. The result was always the same, no matter how the outbursts manifested. My body would completely exhaust itself, and I would collapse. Paramedics have had to revive me more than once."*

Suddenly, Ethan reached across the compartment divide and placed his hand on her wrist, about halfway between her hand and elbow.

"I'm so sorry, Violet. That must be terrifying to go through."

Violet could barely process the words. The moment his hand touched her skin, everything went quiet. Her mind *became hyper-focused on the touch, feeling his skin on hers. The various sounds and smells, lights and shadows in the cabin all disappeared. It was as though they had been transported somewhere else. She could see that nothing had changed, and if she wanted to, she could listen for the sounds or focus on the images, but her mind locked completely and totally on Ethan.*

She also knew that somewhere deep in the back of her brain, she was scrambling to understand, to find a reason, an answer for this complete and utter change. It had to be something physical, perhaps chemical, between them. Whatever it was, it was more than pleasant.

Perhaps it was the pause in conversation, or the confounded look on Violet's face, but suddenly Ethan pulled his hand back.

"I'm sorry," he said. "I didn't mean to . . ."

Violet's right hand shot out and gripped his hand, pulling it back to her wrist before she could even formulate the thought. "No, don't . . ." she said, and let the rest of her thought fade as his hand once again rested on her wrist.

After a few moments of silence, she said, "It took a while, but my team in Zurich finally found a way . . . well, more than one actually, for me to help my brain so that it doesn't overload like that as much. I'm able to better compartmentalize so that my brain doesn't get too full."

"So, the drugs helped you do that?" Ethan said.

Violet could feel the words through his hand as much as hear them from his lips. "Actually, it was more the therapy side that helped. I used to think of a glass jar inside my brain and data as marbles. As more and more marbles come in, the jar would expand and get bigger and bigger to hold them all. It was exhausting.

"But then they showed me how to move marbles out of the jar. So, I have smaller jars all around, and I can put things that are important into other jars to look at later."

"But wouldn't that mean you just have an ever-increasing number of jars instead or one that gets bigger and bigger?" Ethan asked.

Violet smiled because he understood. So few people did. *"That was the second big breakthrough. My team helped me figure out how to cut out the bottom of the main jar."* She looked over at him and saw Ethan half tilt his head to the side. *"I no longer fill up the main jar. If I don't move the marbles to other jars, then they just fall out of the bottom."*

"So, they go away forever?" he said.

"Sort of," Violet answered. *"It's hard to explain, but mostly, I don't think about those things anymore."*

Ethan leaned closer. *"So, the marbles, the data, that you put in the other jars, they're there forever?"*

"Yes," she answered, *"unless I move them back to the main jar."*

"What kinds of things do you put into the smaller jars?" he asked.

"It depends. Sometimes it's just a way to sort out data if there's a lot going on around me and I need to keep from being overloaded. Sometimes it's things I don't want to forget."

She looked over at him, and anticipating his question, she said, *"I can tell you that the first day we met at the café in London, you were wearing a white button-down shirt with eight buttons. The shirt had eighteen different wrinkles in the front, and two frayed threads on the right cuff. Your black slacks hadn't been pressed, though they had a previous crease and there were also two stains. One was likely from your coffee because it looked fresh; the other probably from your last meal because it looked like either a sauce or maybe dried egg. Your shoes hadn't been polished in weeks, and you tend to walk on the outsides of your feet. Your socks were old because they were bunching down around your ankles, and you looked like you hadn't slept in several days. Your hair was washed, but you hadn't been to get it cut in at least a month. But your smile made your dimples show, and despite lack of sleep your eyes were full of kindness. You missed three spots when you shaved that morning, and your nails needed trimming."*

Ethan's eyes widened, and there was a hint of moisture in the corners.

The cabin attendant began turning down the lights, indicating that it was time to go to sleep, and they both began prepping for the night.

Chapter 18
Anders

We exited customs at the Göteborg Landvetter Airport, Sweden's second-largest international airport (after Stockholm Arlanda, of course). As we exited customs, Violet approached a tall man with light red hair and a big smile on his face. He embraced her warmly, lifting her off her feet.

Setting her back down, he looked over at me and extended his hand. "And you must be Ethan?" His accent was thick and Scandinavian, though I couldn't identify which country.

I nodded and shook his hand. "I'm Anders," he said. "Anders Kindberg."

"Anders is Danish, not Swedish," Violet said by way of clarification as she hooked an arm through his and we set off toward the exit, "but he came all this way so that we would have more time together."

Anders looked over at me on his other side. "This is the least I could do. I owe Violet more than I will ever be able to repay." Then, turning back to her, he said, "I actually came up last night and stayed in a hotel so that I would be in time for our trip."

"Trip?" I said before I had time to stop myself.

"We have a bit of a drive, I'm afraid. Unfortunately, there are no direct flights from Singapore to our Malmö Airport. Göteborg is the closest one."

Violet chimed in, "We could have flown straight into Copenhagen, but Anders wanted you to experience the Øresund Bridge, and this way we will have plenty of time for you to learn the final pillar."

Anders led us to a parking lot where a gleaming Volvo sedan awaited us. Violet suggested I get in front with Anders, but I declined and took the back. Soon we were out of the airport and headed down the E6 straight to Malmö, which he said would take roughly two and a half hours depending on traffic and construction.

The drive was very scenic. We passed through several coastal towns and had occasional views of the Kattegat. Anders served as a tour guide, pointing out places we should stop and visit if we came back.

Much of the drive, however, was taken up with learning the final piece of Violet's Humanagement system. "It may surprise you," Anders began, "that the final piece of the Humanagement system is what Violet calls the Happiness Quotient."

I have to admit, it took everything I had not to roll my eyes. Anders was looking in the rearview mirror as he said this; I tried my best to keep a straight face, but inside I could feel myself being disappointed. Despite the endless acronyms, the other pillars had been true learning experiences with a direct impact on how my company could evolve. But happiness? As soon as Anders looked back to the road, I shook my head and let out a quiet sigh.

Violet, in her inevitable way, interrupted my thoughts. "Did you know that Sweden and Denmark have been in the top ten happiest countries in the world for over a decade?"

I knew Scandinavian countries were often ranked as having the happiest people, but I didn't realize it had been over such a long period. Anders, still smiling, continued.

"There are many reasons for this, but since we are focusing on Humanagement, we will talk about how to apply the Happiness Quotient to work, yes?"

I knew his question was more a mechanism of his way of speaking, but I nodded just the same and he began his lesson.

"In 2009, Vishen Lakhiani, the CEO of Mindvalley, gave a talk at the Engage Today conference in Canada that was heralded as one of the best talks of the event. Which was saying something because there were a lot of 'stars'"—he made air quotes with one hand—"speaking at that conference."

"The main point of his talk was what he called getting people into flow. The concept is to have people who are happy in the present—meaning they are happy with their lives and work, *and* they also have goals or a vision of where they want to be in the future.

"One mistake people make when they think of being happy is that this means they have everything they want and thus have reached some sort of plateau. Lakhiani was saying that you can be happy and still want more, and that when people are in this state of both enjoying where they are and also looking forward to where they want to be, this is when they have the most success. In fact, the title of his talk was 'Why Happiness is the New Productivity.'"

"Yeah," I said, "I know there's been a lot of stuff about happiness in the workplace over the last several years and I get it—Google, DreamWorks, Pixar or whatever—but I just don't see how giving people snacks, letting them play video games or ride scooters in the office, and providing whatever other perk of the month is big these days helps the company."

Anders looked over at Violet, whose head was, as always, in constant motion as she surveyed the passing countryside. Their eyes met briefly before Anders glanced into the rear-view mirror and met mine. "Yes, that is what most people think of when they think of happy employees, but it's not what the Happiness Quotient is all about."

I raised my eyebrows slightly as he continued, "Don't worry, there are some perks we can talk about, but they are not the important component."

At that point, he transitioned into tour guide mode as we passed through a few small towns, and he pointed out all the interesting things that should be seen, such as medieval architecture and exclusive clothing and designer shopping areas.

Eventually, he said, "When it comes to the Happiness Quotient, there is a lot more to it than perks. As you've already learned, people leave jobs for many reasons, but the primary one is that they do not feel valued or respected."

I nodded, and then I remembered what Meiying Li had said to me just two days earlier: "The point is, Ethan, that a Culture of Passion and Purpose is so much more than simply finding joy in your work. You will cover some of that in the final Pillar."

"Yes," I responded, "and I know that the Culture of Passion and Purpose is more than just finding joy, which is why I'm still unsure of how this happiness thing fits in."

"It's not about the perks but about how employees are treated by their leaders and the people they work with," Anders said. "What many organizations have failed to understand is that the workforce has changed. At some companies, the employees intuitively know this. The industrial age of workers who stayed at a company their entire careers is no longer."

I nodded. Finally, something we could agree on. Even I knew that "career" workers who did one thing all their lives were a dying breed, if not already extinct.

Anders continued, "Although companies no longer expect loyalty from their employees, they have also stopped being loyal to them."

I frowned a little, unsure of where he was going.

"The prevailing thinking at most organizations is something along the lines that since employees will no longer stay for long periods, the company must get the most out of them while they are working and then discard them. Then they hire the next one to replace the first."

Anders glanced in the rearview to make sure he had my attention. "This has led to a culture of burning out workers at a higher rate than ever before. This constantly connected workforce must overproduce to succeed and can never be 'off,' because they must constantly produce or be replaced.

"This," he pointed out, "is hardly conducive to an atmosphere of happiness."

I couldn't argue with him there, but I was still waiting to hear how happiness fit into this quotient or equation or whatever this pillar was about.

We were more than halfway down the coast of Sweden by now, and again Anders pointed out famous museums and nature parks that were worth visiting. I wasn't sure how famous they were, as I hadn't heard of them, but they were apparently great tourist attractions.

Moving on, he said, "Do you know about TED Talks, Ethan?"

"Yes, of course. I have seen a few online."

"Well," he continued, "in 2018, TED began a video series of their own named 'The Way We Work.' It has something like six seasons of videos now, all with information they gleaned from talks over the years and their own research on best practices for how work is changing and how companies should adapt."

At this point, he looked over at Violet again. "They could have saved themselves a lot of work just by talking to Violet." She smiled briefly at him before looking out the window again.

"When I was talking about how companies are trying to get the most productivity out of employees before they move on, what are they focused on?" he asked.

I smiled, finally knowing the answer to a question. "The bottom line."

"Correct," he said, "or more precisely, they are worried about how much revenue an employee can generate. Given that they believe the employee will last only three to maybe five years, it is no wonder they try to get as much out of them as possible, no?"

Again, he ended with a question that I knew he didn't want me to answer.

"Of course, you have learned that we should not focus on the bottom line," he said.

It was said matter-of-factly, but this time he actually was asking me. So, I replied that yes, I knew well that focusing on the bottom line was not how Humanagement worked.

"Well," he said, "for a moment, let us do the opposite. Let us talk about the bottom line."

My eyebrows rose slightly in surprise.

"Some of the information TED discovered in their series may surprise you. Did you know that organizations with happy employees have three times the revenue growth compared with those that do not have happy employees?" Then he added, "And those same organizations outperform the stock market by a factor of three."

Anders wasn't finished. "Another measure of success organizations focus on is turnover. Did you know that organizations with happier employees have *half* the turnover that companies with unhappy employees have?

"Also, companies lose thirty-two days of productivity each year because of employee depression." He waited a moment to let all the information sink in. "You see, Ethan, even if we did focus on the bottom line, it makes more financial sense to focus on employee happiness."

I nodded slowly as my beliefs about employee happiness began to shift in my mind. Even so, I still had questions. "OK," I said, "but I just don't see how it's possible. I mean, even I don't like every aspect of my job. There are some things I just have to do whether or not I like them."

I could see a big grin on Anders's face in the rearview mirror. "That is an excellent point, Ethan," he said. "And it leads directly into what I want to discuss next, but let me also say this. Having happy employees is not about the tasks they must perform to accomplish their work."

That made me sit back a little in my seat, and I'm sure he could see my confused expression.

"One important aspect to remember is that people cannot be what they cannot see," he said.

I tilted my head a little sideways. I was still trying to understand what he was saying when he added, "In order for your employees to be happy, they must see that *you* are happy. You must live your own values in the company. How can you expect them to be happy if all they see is frustration, stress, and anxiety from you every day?"

As I took in what he said, I thought, *Easier said than done, buddy.*

"One other thing 'The Way We Work' TED series talks about is that while the rate of people who are happy at work is rising globally, it is still lower than it was in the

1980s and '90s. Again, this is because although workers have changed, companies have not."

We were approaching Malmö now, and suddenly I could see in the distance a bridge that seemed to dive into the water. This was the famous Øresund Bridge. Anders had again switched to acting as our tour guide as we turned onto the bridge. "This is a double-track bridge. We drive on the upper level, and a train drives below us."

As we passed between the tall masts of the cable-stayed bridge, I could see that we were approaching land. The land, however, was not the shores of Denmark but an island, and the road we were driving on seemed to disappear into the ocean.

Anders continued, "The island is called Peberholm, and it links the bridge and tunnel. The island is man made and was constructed from material dredged from the seabed in the building of the bridge and tunnel."

As we followed the bridge road, it slipped down into the center of this small island and disappeared into a tunnel under the sea. "The flora and fauna on the island have been allowed to develop freely and undisturbed," Anders said. "Biologists have identified more than five hundred species of plants, and it is a natural habitat for the rare green toad."

It really was a marvel to see.

As we entered the tunnel, Anders brought us back to the task at hand. "The question you are surely asking," he said, "is how do organizations create and keep happy employees?"

"Yes," I answered, "as a matter of fact I am."

"If we think back to the number one reason people leave an organization, that points to why they are unhappy enough to leave. Thus, the opposite would be true of how to make them happy, no?"

This time, he was actually asking the question.

"That makes sense, I guess," I said.

"Following this line of thought," Anders said, "the way to having a culture of happy employees is through trust and respect. An employee who feels trusted and respected will be happy in their work.

"Now, you have already learned many ways this can be done in earlier pillars of Humanagement, especially the Transication and Funambulist Management components."

I nodded in agreement.

"Even with the Hiring and Firing pillars—if you are hiring the right people for the right job, you have already taken a big step in having a happy employee," Anders said. "The next logical step is to trust them."

I frowned a little. "What do you mean?"

"It's simple," he said. "If you have the best person for a particular job as an employee, then you should give them the authority to do the right thing. Trust that they will do the right thing for the organization."

Once again, he let the words sink in. We emerged from the tunnel and were now on the Danish mainland, near the capital of Copenhagen. We stayed on the city's southern outskirts, however, and began driving even further south on the E47.

"The role of management should not be to micromanage employees in every task they do. Yet, every time the workforce or work model changes, what is the first thing that happens?" Without waiting for an answer, he said, "Take the hybrid work model. What was the first thing companies worried about when people began working from home?"

I thought about it for a few moments and said, "They worried that productivity would suffer."

"Exactly," Anders said. "We do not spend every moment of every day wondering if the employee in a cubicle is being their most productive, but move that cubicle somewhere else, for instance to a remote location, and suddenly we think the employee will perform less well."

"Yes, but I'm sure that is based on data that shows a drop in performance."

"I am not aware of such data," Anders said, "but let us suppose that is the case. What does that tell you?"

I sat back thinking, aware that he was looking in the rearview mirror at me. After a moment he added, "Does it tell you that the moving of the work desk caused the drop in performance?"

I realized where he was going and said, "No, it's because the employee was either not in the right position or perhaps not at the right company."

"That is exactly correct," he answered as though he were a proud teacher.

Violet spoke up. Since she had been quiet for so long, her voice was unexpected. "This goes back to the first pillar. If you hire the right people, trust them, help them be as successful as they can be, then the Happiness Quotient takes care of itself. If, however, you need to make a change on your staff, this is where helping the unhappy employee to move on is so important."

My head was swimming with all the connections. Not for the first time, I was amazed at how all the pieces fit so easily together in what I had always thought of as separate components to managing people.

Violet looked out at the landscape of Denmark, her eyes moving constantly as she continued, "What you want, Ethan, is to create a great company to be *from*." After a pause she added, "When someone leaves, they will become an ambassador for your company, and you will never have trouble finding the best employees again."

After driving a while in silence, Anders said, "The other half of this is respecting your employees. This is what some often mistake for trying to solve the work–life balance."

"What do you mean by 'mistake trying to solve'?" I asked.

"Well, if you search the internet for work–life balance or even workplace happiness, first you will find many of today's so-called 'experts'"—he lifted one hand off the steering wheel to create air quotes—"saying this is all the wrong approach. However, for those who believe there should be a work–life balance, they will come up with all sorts of rules and suggestions for trying to accomplish this.

"One of the most often-used quotes, especially among those who are entrepreneurs, is that if you love what you do, you'll never work a day in your life."

I smiled. I had definitely heard this one before.

"Of course, you will find an equal number of people disapproving of this precept and saying it is all untrue. The problem is that both arguments are about making work and life equal." He paused for a moment before continuing, "When we work, we are doing something with our minds, our passions, our skills that we rarely do when we are living our lives outside of work."

I thought about what he was saying, and it made sense. I had just never thought of it that way before.

Anders continued, "So, it is not about our approach to work and life being equal. However, there is something very true about the saying that we should not work to live or live to work. The balance we should be seeking is that we dedicate time for living and time for working. Sometimes those will be more in balance than at other times, but we need to focus on both equally.

"There is nothing wrong with providing perks in an office. A way of making the workday more relaxed, more palatable, more fun. There are many ways to make the tedium of work aspects better. Things like having stand-up meetings to keep them shorter can be a great way to make meetings more productive and less painful. And having nap pods, for example, can make people much more productive during the day."

"Nap pods?"

"I am sure you're familiar with countries that shut down in the middle of the day for people to go home and rest, no?"

I nodded.

"Spain and Italy are famous for doing this," he said, "but you may be surprised to know that Greece, the Philippines, Mexico, Costa Rica, Ecuador, and Nigeria are also countries that have versions of this same concept."

I half laughed because I had no idea so many countries had the concept of a siesta in their culture.

Anders said, "This concept began as a necessity in some parts of the world, where, in the afternoon, the heat reaches its peak and it becomes too hot to be outside. So, people went home after a midday meal to rest until the heat became more bearable. Since then, it has evolved to meet other needs.

"In China, for example, workers are expected to take a short nap at their desks after lunch. Japan even has chairs that turn into cots or recline so much that they are practically a bed for people to take naps in during the day. These companies have found that their employees are more productive when they do this."

I sat silently, taking it all in. I didn't know these practices existed in the working world.

"The point is," Anders continued, "perks come in many forms, and there are no right or wrong ones if those are the things your employees find beneficial. The thing is, taking into account both the Transication and Culture of Purpose pillars, involve your employees in determining what perks will make their lives at work better. Don't assume for them."

After another lengthy pause, Anders spoke again. "The biggest part of the respect aspect of the Happiness Quotient is not the perks. It is about respecting your employees as adults and as individuals."

I shook my head slightly. "What does that mean?"

"It means recognizing that while they are your employees, they are also people, with friends, family, and lives to live outside of work."

Catching my eye in the rearview mirror, he said, "How can you expect someone to respect your company as an employee while they are at work if you don't respect their life as an individual outside of work?"

I mulled that over as we drove, then Anders broke into my thoughts with, "Every organization must set its own policies and values, and they should do so with input from the employees themselves.

"One thing to consider is having on and off limits," he said. Before I could ask, he added, "This means setting communication limits after work. For example, at my company, we very specifically do not have an 'always on' culture where employees are expected to be reachable via text or to be checking email while away from work. In fact, it's quite the opposite. Our policy is that we do not want employees checking emails from 6 p.m. until 7 a.m. the next day, and at no time over weekends."

I opened my mouth, but as if reading my thoughts he added, "This is not always possible for companies who have 24/7 operations for example, or that provide products and services seven days a week, but the point is to have procedures that respect employees off time, whenever that is."

I nodded my understanding, and then Violet spoke up again. "It's equally important to communicate your policies to your partners and customers from the very beginning.

If you don't set expectations early and clearly, the policies won't work, because while those in the organization follow the policies, if those outside constantly violate them then you might as well not have them."

I hadn't even considered how customers and partners played a role in these types of policies. I shook my head, realizing that the more I learned, the more I had to learn.

Anders turned off the highway, and soon we were pulling into a parking lot for something called Camp Adventure.

Chapter 19
Happiness Quotient

*V*iolet had been content to listen for most of the journey down from the airport, occasionally adding a thought or two when it seemed appropriate. Riding in the car had been a little like riding on a train; she could just look out the window and take in the changing landscape as it flashed by. Her ever-hungry brain absorbed everything while she listened to the conversation, dissecting every nuance of Ethan and Anders's unique speech patterns.

Something else had been intruding on her thoughts, however. Back on the plane, when the time had come for them to sleep, she and Ethan had changed and repositioned their chairs into the flat position. Violet had moved as close to the partition as she could. Ethan had too, and then he had lowered the partition to say good night. He had placed his hand over it and rested it against her arm, and she had taken her other hand and placed it on his.

She lay there without moving for almost thirty minutes, afraid that if she moved a muscle, he would move his hand *away. Eventually he began snoring and turned over, taking his hand with him.*

Even without his touch, she had managed to fitfully go to sleep, and for the first time on a plane in as long as she could remember, she slept for over four hours.

Anders explained that Camp Adventure was an incredible place for people of all ages to reconnect with nature. It had everything from pick-your-own flower fields to Denmark's largest outdoor climbing park, with eleven courses. Violet, seeing the fear in my eyes, assured me we wouldn't be doing that.

My fears, however, were not completely assuaged as Anders handed us VIP lanyards created for Violet and me. "Make sure to take the alternate path back from the Forest Tower so you can get to your glamping tent. Yours is called 'Cool Gray,' and I'll go now and drop off your luggage."

He gave Violet a hug and shook my hand, saying he would be back tomorrow to collect us.

I tried to ask what the Forest Tower was, never mind the glamping tent, but he just smiled, waved, and got back in his car. Violet headed toward what looked like the entrance, and I followed warily along.

After sailing through the entrance with our VIP badges, we got onto the boardwalk, where a sign indicated that the 3.2-kilometer raised footpath would lead us to the Forest Tower. The path was made of beautiful wood. It was raised off the forest floor and wound in and around the forest and over streams. The weather was overcast and cool, and although we weren't the only guests, there were stretches where we were alone with the sounds of nature in this beautiful forest.

Violet refused to answer my question about what the Forest Tower was, other than to tell me it wasn't dangerous. Instead, she asked if I had questions about the final pillar in Humanagement. I knew she was just trying to take my mind off what I could only imagine was my impending doom at the Forest Tower, but I played along.

I asked if she had ideas for how to implement the Happiness Quotient. Her answer was vague.

"Every company must do it their own way, but aside from what Anders talked about, there are lots of different ways to help employees while they're at work. Some companies have specific meetings at the beginning and end of each week. At the beginning, they highlight everything that went right the previous week. This is counterintuitive for some people because, typically, Monday meetings are about what needs to be done in the coming week or what didn't get done the previous week."

I nodded because not only did my company do that, but I had been a part of other companies that did the same thing.

Violet continued, "The purpose of this type of meeting is to be grateful for something. It can be work related or not, though that's often how it ends up because the focus is on what happened the previous week that was positive. What's amazing is that someone says they are grateful for a sale they made, or a new product launch or what have you, and everyone in the company gets to share in that gratitude. Then it goes around the room, and everyone has to come up with one thing they're grateful for. Can you imagine starting each week that way?"

I thought some people might find it a little too touchy-feely, but I could see how it would change the mood of traditional Monday mornings.

"Then," she said, "on Fridays they have a different meeting."

A couple walking in the opposite direction passed us and waved, grinning from ear to ear. I watched them go as Violet said, "Before I get to the Friday meetings, let me talk about the 40/5 Rule."

I looked at her questioningly.

"The 40/5 Rule is something several companies I know have instilled. It goes back to the respect component, in that they respect that employees are trading their time for employment and compensation, but that doesn't mean the time is endless. The rule is a value they instill, that employees can only work a maximum of forty hours per week."

I definitely raised my eyebrows at that one. "Whoa, hold on, only forty hours? That will never fly!"

Violet didn't hesitate. "Why not?"

"Well," I said, "I don't know anyone who works less than sixty hours a week, and some longer."

"Why?"

"Why?" I said. "Because it takes that long to get things done."

"Then you're doing it wrong."

"Excuse me!" I said, stopping and turning toward her.

"If it takes sixty hours a week for someone to accomplish their tasks, then you need more people, not more time for the people you have." I opened my mouth to argue, but she cut me off. "More likely, however, is that your people are not productive enough."

I shook my head. "Hold on," I said. "You can't have it both ways. How can they not be productive enough working sixty hours a week, but you want them to work fewer hours?"

Violet turned and started walking again. "What I'm saying is that if you have the right people in the right jobs, and those people feel respected and appreciated and trusted, then forty hours a week would be more than enough for them to accomplish their tasks. If they take sixty, then it's possible they are not being productive enough, which means something is off."

I opened my mouth again, but I couldn't think of how to argue the point.

It didn't matter anyway; she wasn't finished. "Which brings me to the 'five' part. Along with the forty-hour-a-week maximum, the second component is that five of those hours must be spent learning something new."

"This is that hobby stuff Meiying talked about, right?" I said exasperatedly.

"It means they must do something other than their normal work. They can learn a new skill, volunteer for another organization, take a class, anything that expands their knowledge and sparks creativity."

I stopped again. "You're telling me that for over half a day, every week, I should pay my employees to . . ." At this point, I threw up my hands. "I don't know; have fun instead of working?"

Violet smiled, turned, and started walking again. "I'm not telling you anything, Ethan. You asked for ideas, and I'm giving you some that other companies have implemented."

"And you're telling me this actually works for them?" I said.

"Yes, and it works very well. I would venture to guess that if we looked at the data, their employees accomplish more in thirty-five hours every week than yours do in sixty."

Skeptical didn't begin to describe what I was thinking, but another part of me was saying that if Violet was willing to bet on data, I would likely lose that bet.

"That brings me back to the Friday meetings. Usually these happen in the morning because the five hours often take place on Friday afternoons."

"Of course they do," I said sarcastically. "That way people can just start their weekends early instead of doing whatever hobby they are supposed to do."

Violet ignored me and said, "The Friday meetings are teaching moment meetings."

She looked over at me, but I just waved my hand for her to go on.

"The teaching moments are done by the staff, not the management. Each week, one or two employees teach everyone at the meeting something new they learned during their five hours over the past few weeks. It might be a new marketing tip they learned at a seminar, something new they read in a book, et cetera. Really anything."

We crossed over a beautiful bubbling stream as Violet continued, "There are other things you can do, but it all comes down to taking away the things people generally stress about at work. Take your company, for example."

Now I was all ears. Finally, she was getting to something more specific.

"You know how the Transication pillar is about open and honest communication?"

I nodded.

"Your employees would have benefited if you had been open and honest about how things were going financially instead of hiding it from them, but, you know, that's water under the bridge."

"Wait," I said, pointing down at the stream below us, "did you just make a joke?"

Violet didn't even crack a smile. "I'm just saying it's too late to change that now. The point is, one company went even further. Instead of giving out bonuses at the end of the year, they became really transparent about revenue by pledging to give 12 percent of gross profit back to the employees at the end of each year. Not instead of raises but in addition to them. Talk about buying into the company. Every employee knows that the work they are doing will benefit them at the end of the year. In a really good year, the employees might double their salaries."

A sign told us we were getting really close to the Forest Tower. As we rounded the next bend in the path, it came into view, and I stopped. I could feel my heart begin to beat faster, and my throat go dry. Violet had continued walking and now stopped, turning around. I could see in her expression that what she could see on my face was more than fear—it was pure terror.

Chapter 20
The Forest Tower

Violet turned toward Ethan. His face was getting paler by the minute. She gently approached him.

"Ethan, look at me."

He slowly lowered his head and met her gaze. She reached out and took hold of his hands. "You can do this. I will help you. We're going to do it together."

--- • ∞ • ---

Every part of me was shaking. The Forest Tower was massive. (Later, I would learn that it was forty-five meters tall.) It looked like a giant hourglass made of steel and wood, an elaborate crisscross pattern of beams with wooden rings. Wide walking paths wound their way around, and up, the structure. Twelve circles of these paths ascended to the top, which looked like it touched the sky far above the tops of the trees.

The boardwalk flowed into the beginning of the first ramp ring. The path was quite wide and had steel railings on both sides, like endless banisters that wove around and around the tower.

I don't know what it was about Violet's touch, but something made me want to go with her. Not that my fear went away; it didn't. My heart was pounding at just the thought of going up this monstrous structure, but I also didn't want to let go of her hand.

We walked closely side by side, our shoulders touching. Violet stayed on the outside, against the steel banister, allowing me to walk in the middle of the ramp, which was wide enough for three or four people.

There weren't too many other people, though occasionally someone would come down past us or walk past us going up, given that we were moving slowly.

When we'd made it through three rings, the bottom floor of the forest already seemed smaller, and I noticed the rings were also shrinking. We were moving toward the center of the hourglass shape, and with it closer to the massive birch trees that grew in the center of the structure.

There was something calming about getting closer to them. By the time we reached ring six, I had stopped looking down for fear I might collapse. Amazingly, the trees in the center now practically touched the inner banisters. I'm not sure how Violet managed to get me there, but suddenly I was gripping the railing with one hand and touching the side of one of the trees with the other.

The rest of the journey was much more difficult. The higher up we went, the wider and further apart the rings became. Finally, we emerged onto ring twelve.

I was hanging on to Violet's entire arm now, visibly afraid. We were indeed above the tree line, and the view would have awed me, were it not for the fear coursing through my veins.

Violet told me we didn't have to walk around the full 360 degrees of the top ring, but I was determined now to do it. I'm sure there was a part of me that wanted to prove something to her, but it was also for me.

My fear was not about the structure itself. I wasn't afraid that it would somehow collapse. My fear was simply that I might fall. That someone would push me over the railing and I would fall. That was it. Never mind that these banister-type railings were made of steel and came up above my waist. The fear was ever-present.

As long as I could stay in the middle of the path, much to the consternation of people I refused to yield to when they tried to pass us, I could do it.

At one point, Violet pointed. "See that? That's Copenhagen over there, and beyond it you can see a little of the bridge going to Malmö."

It was truly a spectacular vantage point. For a moment I allowed myself to appreciate the view of the tops of the trees, something I would never have thought I would get to see.

As we began our descent, I thought I would be equally afraid as when we had come up, but somehow, holding on to Violet, listening to her tell me all about the tower, I was no longer fearful.

I began to appreciate the view from the surrounding forest, because with each step I knew we were getting closer to the ground.

———— • ≫⊙ • ————

Violet had been so focused on helping Ethan overcome his fear of heights as they conquered the Forest Tower that she didn't realize until they were halfway down that the entire time, her mind had been quieted. She was completely focused on her conversation with Ethan, on helping steady him.

She wasn't trying to distract him as much as help him overcome the fear, embrace it, and still get past it. She was simply a tool to help him do it, but he was doing it on his own.

Every thought she had, everything she said, every moment was simply focused on helping him. Of course, she noticed the scenery, the people they came across, the sounds and smells, but those things were simply going into the jar and out the bottom in her mind. She had no need to catalog or process the data. She could just exist in the moment.

This was such a new feeling for her, it took her a second to realize Ethan had asked her a question.

Smiling and gripping his hand on her arm with her other free hand even tighter, she reengaged in the conversation.

Back on the boardwalk on the forest floor, they did as Anders had said and took the path opposite the one they had come here on. This one went back through the forest towards the entrance from the original path. Suddenly they came upon a row of structures.

Each was part cabin, part Mongolian yurt. The round, tentlike structures were connected to a wooden cabin. Each overlooked a vast lake. Ethan and Violet soon came to one with a sign that said "Cool Gray."

Violet turned her badge around and pulled out a plastic hotel-style key card. She pressed the badge to the reader, waited for the beep, and opened the door.

I followed Violet into the yurt part, a round tent of sorts with a bed and small kitchen. There were green plants all around, a beautiful skylight at the center of the round roof, and windows into the surrounding forest.

I saw her bags at the foot of the bed. Mine were nowhere to be seen. We went through a door into the cabin part of the structure, where we found a bathroom with a claw-foot tub and a deck overlooking the lake. Up a small flight of stairs was another small room with a bed that had my luggage next to it, and another upper deck overlooking the lake.

Unlike camping in a tent, this "glamping" experience included Wi-Fi, electricity, running water, a kitchen, and a woodstove.

We headed back to the yurt, where we found a cooler that Anders had set next to Violet's suitcases. In it were packages of food and a two-page explanation of how to prepare the meal, along with some appetizers, two bottles of wine, and some water.

We started getting our luggage sorted, preparing clothes for bed and to wear the next day. I repacked everything in my suitcase, as I would head home tomorrow morning.

When I returned to the yurt, I knocked on the door and entered to find Violet unpacking the cooler. We spent the next hour chopping and slicing, sautéing and cooking the fabulous meal that Anders had put together for us.

Surprisingly, we did little talking; instead, we worked with and around each other in the tiny but functional kitchen area, sipping on a lovely red wine whose label I couldn't understand. Each of us reviewed the instruction sheet in turn as we worked on our part of the meal. Occasionally we bumped into each other and laughed.

It was a welcome break from the travel and the deep dive into the work we had been doing. As the main dish was cooking in the little oven, we sat in the wooden chairs on the main deck and looked out at the lake, as did many other glampers along the row of yurt cabins.

I reached out and took hold of Violet's hand. She didn't pull back and laid her head back and closed her eyes, taking a deep breath of the cooling late afternoon air and then sighing it out. I watched her for a while and marveled at how short a time I had known her and yet how long it felt.

Eventually, we went back inside to eat the meal we had prepared. We spoke a little over dinner about the Forest Tower. I admitted how frightened I had been but how proud I felt having done it.

Violet added that she didn't think I would walk around the top ring, and that she would have been content with just getting me to go to the top and back down again. I told her it was because of her that I had done it, and for a brief moment, as she looked down to get another bite of food from her plate, I noticed she had blushed ever so slightly. I didn't want the meal to end, because it meant it would be time to go to our separate rooms for the night.

Violet had been so glad when Ethan had reached out on the deck to take her hand, giving her some respite from the constant thinking. There they sat together in the chairs, overlooking the quiet lake, the sun dropping into the horizon, the sounds of the forest creatures filling the night air.

Most of all, she wondered what would happen after dinner.

Despite not physically touching Ethan during dinner, she realized that just being proximal to him soothed her constantly roving mind. It wasn't the same as touching him, but it helped calm her a little just the same.

They finished dinner, cleaned up, and poured the last of the wine into their glasses. After once again stepping onto the deck, they quickly retreated inside, as the night had gotten surprisingly cooler during their meal.

Looking out through the windows, Ethan sighed. The last of the wine had been drunk, and he said they'd better get some sleep.

Violet didn't answer right away. "They say these glamping huts are heated, but I don't think that woodstove will stay lit all night."

Ethan looked over at her, and their eyes met.

"It probably won't," he said. Then, smiling, he added, "I believe there's some science that suggests two bodies together stay warmer than apart."

"I don't know where you got that science from," she said, "but I think it's a theory worth exploring."

Taking her hand, Ethan led her back through the door into the yurt.

Chapter 21
Colorado

I was once again at an airport getting on a plane. I thought back to that night in the yurt, as I so often did, shaking my head. That had been over fourteen months ago. A lot had happened since then.

I had returned home the next day and was back in my office bright and early the following morning. I sat down with Sam, and together we began mapping out the pillars of Humanagement and how we were going to implement them.

I moved her to my desk the next week, over her protests, and set myself up with my laptop on the round table next to her. I told her that if she was going to take over this company, she needed to be in on the changes we were making from the beginning.

We worked long days over the next several weeks, and at one point, it looked quite bleak. We lost several people, even some we had hoped would stay, the people that we thought we needed to stay. Not everyone was on board with the changes we were making, but we kept moving forward.

One day, late in the afternoon after almost everyone had gone, our finance director came in with a long face. The bottom line, so to speak, was that we were just about out of time. The money I had poured in to keep things going was basically spent, and by the end of the following month, we could no longer make payments against the mountain of debt we had accumulated.

The end of the current month was a little over a week away.

I spoke with Violet often over those weeks, mostly on video calls because she was always on the move. The week before, she had come out to the office to see for herself how things were going.

She and Sam had got on immediately. I would often walk into the office to find them both giggling like teenagers, only to stop and look at me with serious expressions the moment I walked in.

"What?" I would exclaim.

"What?" they would respond in unison, then giggle again.

The night after I talked to the accountant, I called Violet and told her where we stood.

There was silence on the line for a moment before Violet said, "I know things haven't been easy. We knew from the outset that creating the change you need in the short time you have was going to be difficult at best."

I nodded silently.

"When I was there, Sam and I looked at how things were going overall. Outside of what you're doing internally, I mean," she said. "I still think there's a chance it will work. Try not to worry and keep going. It's not over yet."

As motivational speeches go, it wasn't much. But there was always something in the way Violet's voice affected me, and for whatever reason I just believed her.

We started the first week of the following month hoping more than anything that somehow, some way, things would work out. At the end of the month, I met with the finance director again, only this time there was an uncertain look on his face as he entered my office.

Speaking slowly, he said, "I'm not sure how, but it looks like we might have actually made a profit this month."

It wasn't much. It was barely anything, in fact, but it was something. It was the first profitable month we had had in almost eighteen months. The following month it went up a bit more. And again the month after that.

We were nowhere near being out of the woods, but we were going in the right direction.

***

I flew into the mountain town of Vail, Colorado, and hired a car. The driver took me on winding roads and over hills and valleys until we pulled up at our destination. The Life Prism Institute. Violet's company.

I wasn't there to see her, however. I knew she was traveling. I was there to see Jeffery, her father figure.

I had met him a few months earlier when the three of us, Violet, Jeffery, and I, had dinner in Denver. Now I had made an appointment to see him, and I entered the building with more than a brief hesitation in my step.

He greeted me warmly and took me up to his office with its spectacular view of the valley below. After the initial small talk, he waited for the reason I had come to see him.

I told him I wanted to ask Violet to marry me.

He nodded a little, with a thin smile on his face. "I thought this might be coming."

I wasn't sure what to say to that. I told him how much I cared for Violet, loved her, and how happy she made me.

He nodded, then said, "It's funny you say that because we've all noticed a change in Violet for a while now." He waved his hand in that gesture that says something without saying anything. "It's not something most people would notice, but those of us who know her could see it. In fact," he continued, "I'm sure you're aware of those she calls her world family?"

I nodded. "Yes, the people she's worked with over the years in her . . . consulting."

He smiled. "Yes. Violet has never been one to just consult on business. She's always formed bonds with those she helps, and that's why she thinks of them as family. You, in fact, fall into the category as part of the global family."

Again, I wasn't sure how to respond, so I kept silent.

"Anyway, I've had several of them reach out over the past few months, and each one has said the same thing. Or, more to the point, some of them have asked something along the lines of 'What's going on with Violet? She seems different. She seems happy.'"

I felt a jolt go through my body, and I'm sure my face flushed a bit.

At that point, Jeffery's expression changed. His smile vanished, and he leaned forward with his elbows on his desk and his hands clasped in front of his face. "I'm not saying that she'll say yes if you ask her."

I felt the same blood that had flushed to my face beginning to drain away from it.

"And there's something else you need to think carefully about before you ask her." He paused and then continued, "I know she has shared quite a bit of her past with you, and you're well aware of her condition."

I nodded respectfully. "Yes, I am."

"What I'm trying to say, Ethan, is that none of us, not me, not her, not the team in Zurich, knows what the future will look like for Violet."

"I don't understand, sir."

He smiled briefly. "While she is stable now, there's no guarantee she will stay that way in the future." He sat back in his chair, sighing. "All her life we have been adjusting and adapting to the way her brain has changed as she grew up. One adjustment here meant another there. With each success, we would have to deal with an additional side effect.

"The Swiss have been amazing, and they continue to research and test and work on ways to help her, but even they admit that it's somewhat a game of whack-a-mole." Jeffery held his hands with palms up as he said it.

He looked at me and I at him, but I wasn't sure how to respond to what he was telling me.

"Ethan," he said, as if reading my mind, "Violet isn't like most people, as you know, but her exceptionality is even more pronounced when it comes to relationships. If you're asking for my blessing, I have to know that you won't run away the minute things get hard, because I'm telling you right now there will be times when it gets harder than you can imagine."

I took a deep breath, forcing myself to think through my answer carefully.

"Thank you," I said first, "for being honest and for looking after her best interests."

He turned his palms up again in a gesture as if to say 'of course'.

I continued, "I have spent a lot of time over the past year listening and observing Violet. I've done my own research and honestly learned, as much as it is possible to learn without being in your shoes, what it's like to be with someone on the spectrum." I quickly raised my hands with my palms out toward him. "I know she's not like others on the spectrum, so my research has been limited, but I too wanted to get an idea of what this might mean.

"The truth is, sir, I'll probably never know until something happens how hard this could get. I know that. But what I also know is that I have never been happier in my life than when I'm with her. I miss her when she's away. I dread that moment every time I know she has to leave, and I count down the hours and minutes until I can at least speak to her again.

"The point is, I don't want to live without her. I mean without her all the time. I know she will travel sometimes without me, but knowing that she will be coming back to me and not just going home somewhere else . . . I don't know. Maybe none of this makes sense to you, but I just don't want to do what I'm doing without her, and I want to help her with everything she needs or will need. I don't want her doing it alone."

I ran out of words. I still wanted to explain it better, tell him how much I loved her, how just seeing her made my heart flutter, but I couldn't find the words.

Jeffery had his hands pressed together in front of him, his fingers steepled and touching his lips as he rocked gently back and forth in his chair. Finally, he nodded slightly. "Well, Ethan, I can't think of anyone else I'd rather have help her. You have my blessing."

He stood and held out his hand, and I almost bounded out of the chair, shaking it far more exuberantly than was necessary with a huge grin on my face.

As we both turned to leave, I looked at his office credenza, which was lined with framed photographs. In one was a young girl, practically a toddler. "Is that . . .?" I asked.

He turned and picked up the frame. "Violet? Yes, she was maybe four years old here." He handed me the frame. I looked at the bright eyes in the little face staring back at me, and my heart fluttered.

I returned it to him, and he put it back.

Turning back towards the door, I suddenly stopped, frozen in place. I stared intently at one of the photographs at the end of the credenza. I was dumbfounded, my mouth open. I could feel my heart thudding in my chest, and I was short of breath.

Jeffery, seeing what I was looking at, went to the picture and touched the top of the frame.

"That's Violet's father. This was taken a few months before he died. We both dressed up as pirates for a Halloween party." There was sadness in his voice. The kind of sadness that dulls with time but never really goes away.

The photo showed Jeffery in traditional pirate garb and a tricorn hat, his arms around the man he had just said was Violet's father.

I couldn't stop staring. My mind raced back in time to London. To my inebriated self as I stood on the wrong side of the railing of London Bridge.

There in the photo was a man with long blond hair and piercing blue eyes, wearing a billowing white shirt with a black vest over it.

The man who had saved me from jumping off the bridge.

Chapter 22
Go or Run

I looked around for what seemed like the hundredth time. *She's not coming*, I thought. Most of the passengers had already boarded the plane. Now the gate agents were calling up the standby passengers one by one.

I looked at the tickets in my hand.

Maybe, with everything moving so fast at work, I had moved too fast with Violet. Had I misread the signals? Was I the only one who felt the way I did? I went over every moment, every conversation, every text, and every email in my head until they all blended together.

The fact was that she hadn't come. Maybe there was an emergency, maybe she had a problem with her medication, maybe she didn't feel the way I felt about her? Maybe, maybe, maybe.

I looked around one more time. I knew I should turn the ticket in and let them give it to someone else. I looked again at my phone. No text. No email. Somehow, I kept thinking that if I waited just one more minute, she'd be there.

I was out of minutes. I looked over at the desk agent, who raised her eyebrow questioningly and glanced at the gate, then back at me.

I sighed and headed toward her with Violet's ticket.

———— • ∞ • ————

Violet's mind was raging. It wasn't just the mass of people in a busy airport that always set her mind into overdrive. It wasn't the millions of details—sights, sounds, and smells—that were causing her anxiety. It wasn't even the banter between the shoeshine man and his customer, whose stand she was hiding behind.

She glanced once more at the gate just around the corner from her hiding place. She could see Ethan glancing nervously at his phone. She could see from his expression that he was upset.

It wasn't all the data. It was the noise emanating from inside her head rather than coming at her from the outside.

She had been trying to calm them down for days now, the incessant inner voices in her mind that were talking almost as fast as the information she was processing from her surroundings. Her anxiety had started the moment Ethan had suggested the trip. At first, she had ignored the voices and simply used her busy schedule to push the thoughts aside. She knew they were in the back of her mind, but she squashed them by focusing all her attention on the tasks she was performing and the cataloging of the ever-present data coming at her.

Until forty-eight hours ago when those thoughts had suddenly and ferociously jumped into the forefront of her mind.

What are you thinking? *They cried out.* **You can't go with him.**

This is a terrible idea; you and he will NEVER work. *Another voice said.*

She knew intrinsically that this was nothing more than fear, but she had never felt a fear this strong, this insistent, this powerful before. She tried reasoning, arguing, debating with the voices over and over again, and still they persisted.

You have too much to lose. What if it doesn't work out and you have another relapse? What if this one kills you? *A sobering thought she knew she could not ignore.*

No one can handle your situation, *the voices insisted.* Yes, he seems nice enough, but that's why you can't do this to him.

This was the argument that really got to her.

If you really care about him, you have to let him go. It would be cruel to lead him on knowing the inevitable is going to happen. *The voices were softer now, as if knowing how difficult this part was for her, yet they were nonetheless determined.* At some point, it will fall apart. He will get tired of you and your 'awkwardness,' your unusual habits, your . . . YOU.

It was hard to argue with the logic.

Yet, there was more to her anxiety. To be sure, the voices were the biggest contributor. But her glances toward Ethan also gave her pause; seeing his face and the look of defeat was also a factor. They had made so much progress from that first day at the café in London where she first met him at his lowest. Knowing that she was now the cause of his sadness was part of what troubled her.

Go or run away? That was the choice she was battling with in her mind. To go to Ethan and begin whatever it was they were trying to start or run away and hide.

GO or RUN?

GO or RUN?

Every fiber of her was fighting back and forth. She knew what her brain was telling her. RUN. It simply made the most sense. It was the safe, secure, and ultimately kind thing to do, and she knew it. Why, then, was she so angry? Why was this war raging inside her head, the likes of which she had never experienced before?

There was something else.

Violet shook her head violently from side to side, earning a quick glance from the shoeshine man and his customer. What is it? She commanded her brain to focus. What else is bothering me?

That was when she heard it.

There was another voice.

A different voice.

How had she not noticed it before?

There was no answer. Closing her eyes, she asked again, this time with every ounce of energy she could muster. She had to know. Why?

The answer caused her eyes to open wide in astonishment.

It's not coming from us. *The voices raging in her head responded.*

Just like that, she knew.

This other voice was coming from her heart.

With every beat, a growing crescendo took over, banishing the voices from her mind in its wake. Louder and louder, the new voice began to push every piece of data to the side. No longer could she smell the shoe polish or the bread of the nearby restaurant; her eyes barely registered the people walking by from the de-boarding plane, and her ears no longer heard their conversations.

All she could hear was the new voice of her heart. Louder, louder, and louder still. Becoming more and more insistent in its command. Like a chorus with every beat of her heart, it shouted:

GO! GO! GO!

Violet breathed deeply, and then took her first step forward towards her future; towards Ethan.

HABBIT21

HUMANAGEMENT
The 7 Pillars of HABBIT21
Violet's 'Future of Work Human Management System'

PILLAR 1
<u>HIRING</u>

When hiring, always hire the smartest person for a given job. You are hiring someone to do a job you either don't know how to do or don't have the time to do. You want them to be the best person at the job that you can afford. They should be better (smarter) at the job than you. You should be the dumbest person in the room (as it relates to that job).

- A candidate's CV/résumé is a calling card that shows you they have some background in the type of job you are hiring for.

- Looking at résumés allows you to narrow the field to a phone interview, which gives you the first impression of the person. This interview simulates how a potential customer meeting this person for the first time will feel when they talk to them. The big question isn't about their qualifications, but rather, do you *like* this person?

- The phone interview is followed by one or more in-person interviews. Eventually, the final interview by the manager, department head, or CEO should be a conversation that determines whether the candidate is a good fit for the organization *and* whether the organization is a good fit for the candidate.

PILLAR 2
IPF and HICCUPs

- *IPF (Immediate Performance Feedback)*
  - ¤ Annual performance reviews are an outdated way of assessing employee performance. Utilize IPF continually throughout the year.
  - ¤ The key is to *praise publicly and admonish privately*.
  - ¤ When done correctly, there should be no "surprise" when it comes time for bonuses, raises, or even letting someone go, because IPF should make the end result clear long before it happens.
- *HICCUP (Human Interactive Conversations and Constant Updating Principle)*
  - ¤ Although IPF is concerned with performance, the similar concept of HICCUP is more general in nature and concerned with ongoing communication with your employees.
  - ¤ These conversations should happen face-to-face, not via technology.
  - ¤ One component of HICCUP is to update the employees on their purpose, their value, and how they fit into the organization.
  - ¤ The #1 reason people leave an organization is because they don't feel valued. HICCUPs help an employee understand their value in the big

picture. It's important to constantly help them understand that value.

- ¤ This communication helps with staying up-to-date with each employee and what is going on in their lives, both professionally and personally.
- ¤ What happens to people personally will affect them professionally.
- ¤ Helping employees achieve their goals and dreams cannot happen without knowing what those are. Regular, ongoing, informal conversations about how they are doing is the key.

PILLAR 3
FIRING

- *Pull the Band-Aid off!*
    - ¤ Letting an employee go, regardless of the reason, changes their entire world as they know it.
    - ¤ One of the most stressful times in a person's life is getting a new job. When you let someone go, this has just become their priority scenario.
    - ¤ This experience will be much more difficult for the employee than the employer.
    - ¤ Always be kind, but firm.
    - ¤ Do not fall into the trap of explaining or justifying the decision. No amount of explanation will change the outcome, nor will it make the employee feel any better.
    - ¤ (If Pillars 1 & 2 have been implemented correctly, this conversation should not come as a surprise. If it does, it indicates that Pillars 1 and/or 2 are not being implemented correctly.)

PILLAR 4
FUNAMBULIST MANAGEMENT

Like a tightrope walker, focus on the goal while adapting as necessary. Similarly, keep focused on employees while adjusting organizationally, and the people will help reach the goal.

- *Play Human Tetris with employees.* Historically, business leaders have been trying to get the most *out* of their employees instead of helping them get the most out of *themselves.* Like playing the game of Tetris, help employees fit into the best role for them in the organization. Help them understand their talents and strengths, then find where those talents and strengths fit best in the organization.

  - ¤ Human Tetris may also require moving people *outside* the organization. When someone no longer fits within the organization (or the organization no longer fits them), help them find another company *while continuing to employ them.* Assist them while they help train their replacements (thus cutting down on some of the cost of onboarding the new employee).

- *Be the buffer.* A manager/supervisor/boss may not understand the nuances of employees' jobs, lives, goals, and dreams, but their direct manager does. The manager will get credit when things go right (though they should pass that credit on to the people who deserve it), so it's only fair that they take the blame when things go wrong. Not allowing ire to "roll downhill" will also help build trust in the team.

PILLAR 5
TRANSICATION (Transparent Communication)

- *Transication* means being open about everything and having transparent communication in everything.

  - ¤ If Pillar 1 is implemented successfully, then the best people available are in the best positions within the company. They are, in essence, subject matter experts within the organization. Why *not* utilize their expertise?

  - ¤ Engage employees in all aspects of the business, keep them informed, and ask for their help. Being the boss doesn't mean having all the answers. Often it is the very people who do the work that will generate the most creative solutions to the problems the organization faces.

- *SPOOFing (Succeed Publicly and Often, Open about Failure)*

  - ¤ When success happens, give credit where it's due and do it publicly as often as possible. Also, create a culture where it's OK to fail. It's not about getting stuck in failure. Instead, emphasize that it's OK to think out of the box even if something doesn't work out, because it means having learned another way not to do something. There is value in that.

  - ¤ Being open about failure means educating everyone on the team about something that doesn't work, which will eventually lead to the solution that does.

PILLAR 6
COP (Culture of Passion/Purpose)

- *A culture of passion/purpose is more than simply finding joy in work.* Passion and purpose at work are something that exists beyond the individual. It is a two-way street that encompasses both how the employee brings passion to what they do and how the employer builds a culture that fosters passion and purpose.

  - ¤ Helping employees bring passion to what they do can be accomplished through the idea of *passion projects.*

  - ¤ Build a culture that fosters passion and purpose by helping employees understand their noble purpose: the notion that there is something bigger than the company to work for.

  - ¤ A noble purpose can be about finding ways to give back to communities, doing less harm to the planet, or participating in an industry-wide solution to a global problem. It can be anything that excites and bonds employees together. Something to unite the tribe.

- *BAGS: Be a Good Steward*

  - ¤ The true purpose of business is to find solutions to challenges—in other words, to make things better.

  - ¤ When done correctly, business doesn't just solve a problem. It makes everything surrounding the problem, as well as the problem itself, better. It improves a community, reduces the impact the solution has on the planet, or improves the lives of those affected by the solution.

  - ¤ Doing good *is* good for the bottom line. It is possible to be a good steward and give back to the community or the environment and have it be profitable.

PILLAR 7
HQ (Happiness Quotient)
Organizations with happy employees have three times more revenue growth, outperform the stock market by a factor of three, and have half the turnover of other companies.

- *Happiness at work is good for the bottom line.*
  - ¤ Happy employees are a product of trust and respect. When the best person is hired for a particular job, trust that they will do the right thing for the organization. Don't micromanage employees; trust them and help them be the best versions of themselves. These practices result in happier employees, and the byproduct is better performance (i.e., improved productivity and outcomes).
  - ¤ The goal, as with all the pillars, is to be the best company to be *from*. Let previous employees be the organization's best marketing asset.
- *On/Off Limits: Communications (email, text, etc.) & the 40/5 Rule*
  - ¤ Recognize that employees are also people, with friends, family, and live outside of work. Respect the life they live as well as the work they do. *That* is work–life balance. It's not about both being equal but about both being respected and valued.
  - ¤ Don't expect employees to be "on" 24/7, to answer emails on their time off, or to respond to texts instantly, or at all, when they're not working.

- ¤ Being an employee (exempt or not) doesn't mean they should be expected to work more than forty hours per week. If a typical work-week is forty hours and employees are not able to accomplish the work in that timeframe, it may be time to hire more employees.

- ¤ The "5" part of the rule is about helping employees boost their creativity by giving them five hours a week to do something that sparks their creativity and is *not* connected to the work they do. Finally. give them time to share with the team what they have learned from their passion projects.

ABOUT THE AUTHOR

Michael Jenet was born in Belgium and moved to the United States when he was seven years old. He is an eight-year veteran of the U.S. Air Force.

An international best-selling and award-winning author, *A Better Life* was first published in 2015, but was later put out of print by the original publisher. Jenet started Journey Institute Press to keep other authors from having the same fate.

A Better Work is the second book the 'Better' series.

He lives in Colorado with his wife and family.

JOURNEY INSTITUTE PRESS

Journey Institute Press is a non-profit publishing house created by authors to flip the publishing model for new authors. Created with intention and purpose to provide the highest quality publishing resources available to authors whose stories might otherwise not be told.

JI Press focusses on women, BIPOC, and LGBTQ+ authors without regard to the genre of their work.

As a Publishing House, our goal is to create a supportive, nurturing, and encouraging environment that puts the author above the publisher in the publishing model.

Guide Point North Publishing is an Imprint of Journey Institute Press, a division of 50 in 52 Journey, Inc.

NOTE: The world of publishing has changed dramatically. This has also affected authors and their ability to let readers know about their books. Today, most people buy books based on word of mouth. If you would like to help this author, please consider leaving an honest review of this book on retail sites and book community sites.

www.ingramcontent.com/pod-product-compliance
Lightning Source LLC
Chambersburg PA
CBHW042139210326
41458CB00085B/6835/J